ISRAEL AND THE CHURCH

ISRAEL AND THE CHURCH

Two Voices for the Same God

JACQUES B. DOUKHAN

HENDRICKSON
PUBLISHERS

© 2002 by Hendrickson Publishers, Inc.
P. O. Box 3473
Peabody, Massachusetts 01961–3473

Printed in the United States of America

First Printing—March 2002

Library of Congress Cataloging-in-Publication Data

Doukhan, Jacques.
    Israel and the church : two voices for the same God /
Jacques B. Doukhan.
        p. cm.
    Includes bibliographical references and index.
    ISBN 1-56563-616-3 (pbk. : alk. paper)
    1. Jewish Christians. 2. Judaism—Relations—Christianity.
3. Christianity and other religions—Judaism. I. Title.
    BR158 .D68 2002
    261.2'6—dc21
                                        2001008157

CONTENTS

PREFACE: THE TWO JEWS

In dream I saw two Jews that met by chance,
One old, stern-eyed, deep-browed, yet garlanded
With living light of love around his head,
The other young, with sweet seraphic glance.
Around went on the Town's satanic dance,
Hunger a-piping while at heart he bled.
Shalom Aleichem mournfully each said,
Nor eyed the other straight but looked askance.

Sudden from Church out rolled an organ hymn,
From Synagogue a loudly chanted air,
Each with its Prophet's high acclaim instinct.
Then for the first time met their eyes, swift-linked
In one strange, silent, piteous gaze, and dim
With bitter tears of agonized despair.[1]

I will start with the poet Israel Zangwill, with his tension—an un-resolved tension. I will start with his dream—something irreal, for the reality is too hard, too absurd, too unbearable.

He sees two Jews; they are related by nature. They bear the same suffering, carry the same hope, and share the same identity: "two Jews." Yet, they are separated by a tension of two thousand years and stand in stark contrast to each other.

One is old; he has the antiquity, the strength, and the life of the roots. The other is young; he has the charm and the face of the blossoming branch. Around them the poet sees a "satanic dance," as if they were going to be misused and misrepresented. Evil jumps

---

[1] Israel Zangwill, *Moses and Jesus,* in *Dreamers of the Ghetto* (New York and London: Harper, 1898), viii.

around them, plays with them, and deceives the people about them, hiding their true faces. The sounds of music and the shouts of joy burst out "while at heart he bled."

They say to each other, *"Shalom Aleichem."* "Peace on you," a greeting of love and of hope, wishing life and happiness. Yet, there is no peace, no life, no happiness, no love, *because of them.* The greeting is sad; it is said "mournfully."

Two Jews were supposed to generate *Shalom;* and yet, people have taken their names to lie, to hate, and to kill. They do not dare to look straight at each other, lest they there recognize their own pain, their own shame, their failure: "Nor eyed the other straight but looked askance."

Two Jews were supposed to generate Shalom; and yet, people have taken their names to lie, to hate, and to kill.

The second strophe shifts brutally to a more explicit statement: "Sudden. . . ." The partners of the tragedy are denounced: the church and the synagogue, the Jews and the Christians, are called upon. The two peoples, the two great religions are named, each one with its prophet, each one with its spiritual pride, each one with its truth, a truth claimed loud *against* the other truth.

And, therefore, when their eyes finally meet "for the first time," the gaze is silent. Because there is so much to say and because words have become inadequate and out of place, but also because profound emotion is choking them "with bitter tears of agonized despair."

This is my starting point on the Jewish-Christian drama: this sadness, this tension, this "agonized despair." As a Jew, Israel means for me a history that goes far in the past with profound and venerable roots. The history of a God, the eternal God of the universe, who came down and spoke and saved. The history of a people, *my* people, who walked and struggled, a history of suffering and humiliation, and also a history of glories and victories. As a Jew, my heart bleeds and cries when I think of the Holocaust, and it beats and trembles when I think of Eretz Israel. Israel means for me the beauty and the truth of the Hebrew Scriptures, the revolted shouts of the prophets, the high ethical ideals, and the profound wisdom of the sages and the challenge of their questions. As a Jew, I studied these Hebrew pages, loved them to the deepest of my soul, and devoted to them my life as a researcher and a teacher. Israel means for me a brother, a sister, a father, a mother, and a teacher with whom I learned to remember.

What the church means for me, because of history, is loaded with disturbing ambiguities. But in spite of this, I have been able to discover in this testimony the high values and the great truth of "the other young" sung by Zangwill. For me, the church means also dear friends with whom I am working, struggling, and dialoguing, with whom I learned to love and to hope.

I know, the "two Jews" are rarely seen together. This association is either strange or suspect. One cannot redo history, and those who forget it are condemned to betray it. Yet, without forgetting, I cannot ignore what I saw. "I felt myself to be a Jew who was a Christian, a Christian who remained a Jew."[2]

My standpoint is then one of tension, a tension that I bear in my flesh and in my intellectual and spiritual life: I heard the two voices. And it is the weight of this tension that has pressed me to think and study about it, to teach about it, and eventually to write about it. It is the Jewish-Christian tension in my flesh and in my scholarly and professional life that has given birth to this book. In echo to Israel Zangwill, I will set my questions straight: Were Jesus and Moses indeed irreconcilable? Are our theological and historical clichés in agreement with the original intention of prophetic revelation and with what indeed took place in history? Did the Jews reject Jesus? Did Jesus reject Moses? What propelled Christianity beyond the borders of Israel? Or, to

> *My standpoint is then one of tension, a tension that I bear in my flesh and in my intellectual and spiritual life: I heard the two voices.*

---

[2] Anonymous, "When the Wall Is Fallen," *The Atlantic* 176.6 (December 1945): 91–96.

use the words of Rabbi Gilles Bernheim, "Why did Christianity become a non-Jewish religion?"[3]

Just a few years ago, this last question was hardly entertained. But today, after the Holocaust, it is no longer decent for a Christian to deny the Jewish heritage of the church. And after the creation of modern Israel on the very spot where the first events of Christian history took place, it is no longer reasonable for a Jew to question the Jewish setting of Christianity. Jews and Christians have come to recognize their common roots. Does that mean that we are progressing toward Jewish-Christian reconciliation? Is this reconciliation possible? And here I do not simply refer to the success of organized meetings and to the polite smiles of professionals at interconfessional dialogues. I am thinking specifically of Moses and Jesus and what they represent. Even if the tension was not their original intention, even if we can show that Jesus was at home in ancient Judaism and that early Christianity never intended to repudiate the law of Moses, and even if we can show that there was a time when the Jew could be Christian without any tension, the question strikes today more burningly than ever: After two thousand years of sad history and after the Holocaust, is reconciliation between the two Jews, between Moses and Jesus, within the hearts, minds, and lives of Christians and Jews, still possible? All other questions lead to this one; and, indeed, it is the ultimate question of this book.

> *After two thousand years of sad history and after the Holocaust, is reconciliation between the two Jews, between Moses and Jesus, . . . still possible?*

---

[3] Gilles Bernheim, "Dépasser un dialogue de surface," *Le christianisme du XXème siècle* (April 1991): 12. All translations are the author's unless otherwise indicated.

CHAPTER 1

WHEN THEY WALKED TOGETHER

Too often history is distorted because it is viewed from the perspective of our own vision of the present reality. We project into the past what looks familiar to our eyes today. And under the pressure of our habits and the weight of our laziness, we cultivate clichés and prejudices and thus construct a history that better fits our natural inclination.

This observation is particularly true in regard to Jewish-Christian history. From the separation between Jews and Christians that we see now, we assume that it was always so; we conclude that it had to be so. Yet serious consultation of the original documents, the New Testament and the ancient Jewish writings, in addition to the testimony of archaeology and the latest findings from sociology, provide us with a completely different picture: There was a time when Jews and Christians walked together; they worshiped together; they believed and hoped together.

WHEN CHRISTIANS WERE JEWS

In the beginning of the last century, Friedrich Delitzsch (1850–1922) suggested that Jesus was of Gentile extraction and that Christianity had nothing to do with Judaism. This kind of statement was then a mere expression of anti-Semitic movements in pre-Nazi Germany. Today, it is no longer necessary to remind my readers that early Christians were Jews. The Messiah who inspired them, the disciples who followed him, their writings, and their teaching affirmed their Jewishness.

Jewish Messiah

Jesus was born as a Jew. He was circumcised on the eighth day according to the law (Luke 2:21). He received a Jewish name: *Jesus* is the transliteration through the Latin and the Greek of the original Hebrew *Yeshua* or *Yeshu*, a Galilean pronunciation, or more fully *Yehoshua* (like our Joshua), meaning "Yahweh is salvation" or "Yahweh will save." Matthew attests to this Hebrew derivation in his report of the angel's explanation: "You are to name him Jesus, for he will save his people from their sins" (Matthew 1:21).[1] In fact, this name was very common in the first century; Josephus mentions nineteen persons with the name Jesus.[2] This popularity probably reflected the revival of Jewish nationalism in the wake of the Maccabean War and, on a deeper level, the longing of the people for liberation from Roman domination. These names pointed, indeed, to the first person of that name, "Joshua son of Nun" (Joshua 1:1), who led the Israelites to the promised land. Interestingly, the author of the Epistle to the Hebrews attests to that connection, as he uses the name Joshua to refer to Jesus (Hebrews 4:8).

The historical person Jesus was rooted in the flesh of Jewish history. His genealogy is given on the first page of the gospel to establish his Jewish descent: "the Son of David, the Son of Abraham" (Matthew 1:1). Even the rhythm of this genealogy, which plays on the number fourteen (Matthew 1:17), the numerical value of the Hebrew name David (D = 4, W = 6, D = 4), attests to the same Jewish soil of Jesus' birth.[3] As for the Davidic origin of Jesus, it should not be regarded as an anachronism since Davidic families are attested in Jesus' time. An ancient rabbinic source reports that eminent families were entitled to bring wood for the temple altar, and among

---

[1] Unless otherwise noted, biblical quotations are from the New Revised Standard Version.

[2] A. Schalit, *Namenwörterbuch zu Flavius Josephus* (Leiden: E. J. Brill, 1968), 60–61.

[3] This sort of calculation, known as *Gematria*, is well attested in rabbinic circles; it is also used in Revelation 13:17–18 (see also the *Epistle of Barnabas* 9:8, a very early Christian work).

them were listed members of the house of David: "The Wood-offering of the priests and the people was brought nine times [in the year]: on the 1st of Nisan, by the family of Arah of the tribe of Judah; on the 20th of Tammuz by the family of David of the tribe of Judah."[4]

Archaeological evidence also confirms the existence of Davidic families in the first century B.C.E. In a burial cave from this period, discovered in 1971 in Jerusalem, an ossuary bears an inscription saying that the bones placed inside belong to the lineage of David.[5]

Certainly Jesus looked like a Jew and not like a blond, blue-eyed Christian knight of the Middle Ages. He lived in a Jewish territory in first-century Palestine. He studied with his parents, but also with his friends and the teachers (Luke 2:41–47). He spoke a Jewish language, the Jewish Palestinian Aramaic of that time. The authors of the New Testament even remember some of his Aramaic and Hebrew words: when he prays to God, *Abba* (Father; Mark 14:36); when he performs a miracle, *Talitha cum* (Little girl, get up!; Mark 5:41); and when he dies on the cross, *Eli, Eli, lama sabachthani?* (My God, my God, why have you forsaken me?; Matthew 27:46).

He lived as a faithful and practicing Jew. He received a traditional Jewish education. At the age of twelve, he followed the prescription of the Mishnah (*Yoma* 8:4) and visited the sages in Jerusalem. This time was considered crucial in Jewish education. From then on, the male child began to make the transition to adult responsibilities under the Torah: vows became binding, parental punishment could be more severe, and fasting was required for a whole day (*b. Berakhot* 24a; *b. Yoma* 82a). He kept all the Jewish laws and Jewish festivals and ate kosher food (Luke 2:41–43). He attended synagogue where he prayed, taught, and was deemed worthy to "ascend" the *bimah* to read the Torah (Luke 4:16–20).

Jesus' Jewish education is evidenced in the fact that people were accustomed to addressing him as a rabbi ("my teacher"; Matthew

---

[4] *M. Ta'anit* 4:5. All Mishnah quotations are from Herbert Danby, *The Mishnah* (London: Oxford University Press, 1933). Cf. *t. Ta'aniyot* 3:5; English translation by Jacob Neusner, *The Tosefta* (6 vols.; New York: Ktav, 1977–1986, 2.274–75; repr. in 2 vols., Peabody, Mass.: Hendrickson, 2001).

[5] Dan Barag and David Flusser, "The Ossuary of Yehohanah Granddaughter of the High Priest," *Israel Exploration Journal* 36 (1986): 39–44.

26:49; John 1:38; 20:16), a form of popular address commonly used in those days. Interestingly, his profession as a carpenter was another token of his scholarship. Carpenters were considered particularly learned—so much so that the word "carpenter" came to be used as a synonym for "learned man."[6]

As a Jew faithful to the Torah, Jesus wore *tefillin* and *tzitzit* required by Numbers 15:38–41 and Deuteronomy 22:12.[7] This is evidenced by the story of the sick woman who touched the fringe of his garment, that is, his *tzitzit* (tassels), in order to be healed (Matthew 9:20).

As a Jew, Jesus recited the ancient Psalms, but also the traditional *Shemoneh Esreh* (Eighteen Benedictions) and the *Qaddish*—the great prayer of the "Sanctification" of the name of the Lord. The moving *Avinu Malkenu* (Our Father, Our King) inspired his prayers. And the specific words and the same literary forms have been recognized between traditional Jewish prayers and Jesus' prayers, including the well-known Lord's Prayer. It has been pointed out that this prayer "sentence for sentence, phrase for phrase and word for word" can be found in Jewish sources.[8] The Jewish parallels to this prayer have been traced out carefully by Schalom Ben-Chorin, who concludes that "the elements are altogether from the Synagogue; . . . in its simplicity and completeness, this prayer is actually a high point."[9]

Jesus submitted himself to the Jewish custom of *miqveh* and, like many other religious Jews of his time, was immersed in the Jordan

---

[6] Jacob Levy, *Wörterbuch über die Talmudim und Midraschim* (Darmstadt: Wissenschaftliche Buchgesellschaft, 1963), 3:338.

[7] Jesus' objection, recorded in Matthew 23:5, concerns the misuse of *tefillin* and *tzitzit* for ostentation.

[8] Ernest R. Trattner, *As a Jew Sees Jesus* (New York: Scribner, 1931), 74; Brad H. Young, *The Jewish Background to the Lord's Prayer* (Tulsa: Gospel Research Foundation, 1999).

[9] Schalom Ben-Chorin, *Jesus im Judentum* (Wuppertal: Theologischer Verlag, 1970), 41–42.

River, a ritual that the Mishnah defined as the highest grade of cleansing (*m. Miqwa'ot* 1:6).

His works and even his miracles were Jewish. Rabbinic literature is full of stories of rabbis performing miracles, for the Jewish people believed in miracles. Jewish scholar Max Kadushin observes: "Indeed it is hardly an exaggeration to state that the presence of *Nissim* [miracles] was, in a sense, within the expected order of things."[10] When rain was needed, a righteous rabbi shouted at God to end the drought. In one classic story, Choni, the circle drawer, challenged God; he drew a circle in the dirt and stood in the middle of it and declared that he would not move until God answered and rain fell. And God finally answered: it rained (*m. Ta'anit* 3:8; cf. Josephus, *Jewish Antiquities* 14.22–24).

Likewise, Jesus urges his disciples to challenge God and "importune the Father" until he gives up and finally answers the person who prays "because of his persistence" (Luke 11:8). On this matter, the comments of Rabbi Simeon ben Shetah, a leader of the Pharisees, come particularly close to Jesus' theology: "You importune God, and he performs your will; like a son who importunes his father and he performs his will" (*m. Ta'anit* 3:8).

Many miracles delivered the sick, and the similarities between those rabbinic stories and Jesus' performances are often striking:

> Our Rabbis taught: Once the son of R. Gamaliel fell ill. He sent two scholars to R. Hanina b. Dosa to ask him to pray for him. When he saw them he went up to an upper chamber and prayed for him. When he came down he said to them: Go, the fever has left him; . . . They sat down and made a note of the exact moment. . . . at that very moment the fever left him and he asked for water to drink.[11]

This miracle is similar to the case of the centurion's servant who was also healed at a distance (Matthew 8:13).

Jesus' methods of teaching were Jewish. He constantly based his argument on the Hebrew Scriptures. When he criticized certain practices of his time, he used the Old Testament Scriptures to support his charge (Matthew 22:37–40). Even his messianic claim was

---

[10] Max Kadushin, *The Rabbinic Mind* (New York: Jewish Theological Seminary of America, 1952), 157.

[11] *Berakhot* 34b; English translation by I. Epstein, *The Babylonian Talmud* (London: Soncino Press, 1948), *Seder Zera'im,* 1:215–16.

supported by constant reference to the Hebrew Scriptures. On that matter, Jewish scholar Hugh J. Schonfield makes the following remarkable statement: "It is needful to emphasize that neither before nor since Jesus has there been anyone whose experiences from first to last have been so pin-pointed as tallying with what were held to be prophetic intimations concerning the Messiah."[12] Schonfield furthermore acknowledges the existence of the concept of a suffering Messiah in the days of Jesus.[13] Jesus' use of parables to teach important ethical and religious lessons has many parallels—not only with the Hebrew Scriptures but also with the rabbinic midrashim and the rhetorics of that time. Rabbinic literature contains some five thousand parables written mostly in Hebrew,[14] another strong indication that Jesus gave his parables originally in Hebrew.

It is, therefore, no exaggeration to think that unless biblical interpreters possess a knowledge of the rabbinic methods of parables, the messages of the parables of Jesus will be misunderstood.[15] When Jesus refers to the leaven to illustrate his teaching on the kingdom of God, he is using well-known imagery. So, Rabbi Joshua the Son of Levi compares the Hebrew concept of *shalom* (peace) to the action of leaven: "Great is peace, for peace is to the world as leaven to the dough. Had not the Holy One, blessed be He, given peace to the earth, the sword and the beast would have robbed the world."[16] Likewise, Chaya bar Abba compares leaven to the Torah, for it has the same inner power: "Even if they [the Jewish fathers] forsook me, but kept occupying themselves with the study of my Torah, its leaven . . . would be so powerful as to bring them back to me."[17]

---

[12] Hugh J. Schonfield, *The Passover Plot: A New Interpretation of the Life and Death of Jesus* (New York: Geis, 1966), 36.

[13] Ibid., 212.

[14] See David Bivin and Roy Blizzard Jr., *Understanding the Difficult Words of Jesus: New Insights from a Hebraic Perspective* (rev. ed.; Shippensburg, Pa.: Destiny Image, 1995), 73–78.

[15] Cf. Brad H. Young, *Jesus the Jewish Theologian* (Peabody, Mass.: Hendrickson, 1995), 75.

[16] A. Cohen, trans. and ed., *The Minor Tractates of the Talmud* (2 vols.; London: Soncino, 1965), 2:597.

[17] *Pesiqta de Rab Kahana* 15:5; English translation by William G. Braude and Israel J. Kapstein, *Pesikta de-Rab Kahana* (Philadelphia: Jewish Publication Society, 1975), 279.

Even Jesus' humor and irony were essentially Jewish. It has been noticed that "it is through the rabbinic sources that we find the connection between Jewish and foreign contribution to New Testament humour."[18] The way he ridiculed his opponents and the "pious fools" (Matthew 22:19–22) and made use of satire (Matthew 23; Luke 11:39–54) and laughter as a means of education were typical of the Jewish milieu in which he grew up.

When Jesus died, he was buried according to Jewish customs (Matthew 27:57–61). His body was anointed with spices and was wrapped in a linen cloth (John 19:39–40).

Jesus was born, lived, and died as a Jew. And beyond the historical fact, every moment of his earthly existence was given a highly Jewish significance. Also, the theology used to explain the events was Jewish in nature. Jesus was born under the sign of David, which meant in Jewish terms a messianic destiny. He lived as a powerful rabbi. His teachings and his miracles, his religious works and his acts of love received a profound Jewish meaning: He was identified as the one who was presented by the Hebrew prophets to bring *shalom* into the hearts and hope to the oppressed Jewish people. Even his death was interpreted along Jewish categories of thinking. He was associated with the sacrifice of the temple and the lamb of Passover, the very sign of deliverance from slavery. The technical Greek word "exodus," used in Luke 9:30–31 to describe Jesus' death, suggests the redemptive significance of his death. In the same passages, the story of the visitation of Moses and Elijah takes on special meaning. The association of these two prophets has been interpreted as representing the Law (Moses) and the Prophets (Elijah). But in this context, which evokes the exodus, the presence of these two persons should rather be understood in relation to the miracle of salvation. Indeed, they are both mentioned in the Passover celebration; there, Moses is the key actor who leads the people out of slavery, and Elijah is the one who brings along the future eschatological deliverance of Israel. Besides the traditional Haggadah which is recited at *Pesah,* a homiletic midrash has preserved the meaning of this association:

---

[18] Jakob Jónsson, *Humour and Irony in the New Testament: Illuminated by Parallels in Talmud and Midrash* (Reykjavík: Bókaútgáfa Menningarsjóðs, 1965), 251.

Almost every word,

every act of Jesus, every

story about him, and

every interpretation of

his presence has strong

echoes in Jewish

writings and tradition.

You find that two Prophets rose up for Israel out of the Tribe of Levi; one the first of all the Prophets, and the other the last of all the Prophets: Moses first and Elijah last, and both with a commission from God to redeem Israel: Moses, with his commission, redeemed them from Egypt, as is said *So come, I will send you to Pharaoh* (Exodus 3:10). And in the time-to-come, Elijah, with his commission, will redeem them, as is said *Lo, I will send you the prophet Elijah* (Malachi 3:23). As with Moses, who in the beginning redeemed them out of Egypt, they did not return to slavery again in Egypt; so with Elijah, after he will have redeemed them out of the fourth exile, out of Edom, they will not return and again be enslaved—theirs will be an eternal deliverance.[19]

The New Testament contains a multitude of such examples. Almost every word, every act of Jesus, every story about him, and every interpretation of his presence has strong echoes in Jewish writings and tradition.

Jewish Disciples

Not only the Messiah, but also his followers were Jewish. Jesus discipled them in the fashion typical of first-century rabbis. At that time, rabbis gathered around them disciples called *Talmid hakham* (the disciple of the wise), who devoted their lives to the study of Torah and embodied the religious ideal of their master in many respects. Scholarship along with moral qualities were required in a disciple: "Any scholar whose inside is not like his outside, is no scholar."[20] Often

---

[19] *Pesiqta Rabbati* 4:2; English translation by William G. Braude, *Pesikta Rabbati* (2 vols.; New Haven/London: Yale University Press, 1968), 1:84–85. The versification of most English translations of the Bible differs at some points with the verse numbering in the Hebrew Bible. For example, the Hebrew Malachi 3:23 is Malachi 4:5 in the NRSV. We will generally cite the English versification throughout this work, but the reader can find the differences in *The SBL Handbook of Style* (ed. P. H. Alexander et al.; Peabody, Mass.: Hendrickson, 1999), Appendix E.

[20] *B. Yoma* 72b; English translation by I. Epstein, *The Babylonian Talmud* (London: Soncino, 1938), *Seder Mo'ed*, 346–47.

these disciples were called to leave their homes in order to follow their teacher wherever he went. So did, for instance, the disciples of the messianic prophets of the Zealots who followed their master into the wilderness or to the Jordan. Jewish literature speaks of many Jewish sages who were followed by small groups of disciples. Ezra had five disciples (2 Esdras 14:42). Rabban Johanan ben Zakkai was also accompanied by five disciples (*m. Avot* 2:8–9). Several traditions record various numbers of disciples gathering around Rabbi Akiba: five according to one tradition (*b. Yevamot* 62b), seven according to another tradition (*Tanhuma Hayyei Sarah* 6). The disciples were to become intern teachers themselves to be sent to transmit the teaching of their master. The rabbinic term for such a charge was *shaliah* (from *shalah,* "to send"). The *shaliah* was considered a full representative of the master who sent him. As the Mishnah emphasizes, "a man's *shaliah* is like himself"(*m. Berakhot* 5:5).

Likewise, Jesus gathered around himself a group of *shalihim* (apostles) whom he would later send to the world. They were twelve, a very Jewish number, which pointed to the twelve tribes of Israel. All his apostles and disciples were Jewish from all social classes and all horizons. They were priests (Acts 6:7) and Pharisees (John 3:1), but also Zealots (Luke 6:15), tax collectors (Matthew 9:9), and fishermen (Matthew 4:18).

The idea that most of them were little educated is a cliché that ignores the reality of Jewish life.

The idea that most of them were little educated is a cliché that ignores the reality of Jewish life. Not every Jewish child went to the rabbinic school, the *beyt hamiddrash,* but they all received a good religious and theological education. In Jewish society, education was first of all a matter of parental duty. In addition, by the end of the First Temple period, there is evidence of formal religious instruction by the Levites (2 Chronicles 17:8–9).[21]

---

[21] See Fletcher H. Swift, *Education in Ancient Israel, from Earliest Times to 70 A.D.* (Chicago: The Open Court Publishing Company, 1919), 22, 32–34. On the evidence of schools in ancient Israel, see James L. Crenshaw, *Education in Ancient Israel: Across the Deadening Silence* (Anchor Bible Reference Library; New York: Doubleday, 1998), 85–113.

Shimeon ben Shetah, a first-century B.C.E. leader, decreed that all youths of seventeen should receive a formal education (*y. Ketubbot*

When Christians began to receive additional writings, they never intended to set them up as a separate entity to replace the other Holy Scriptures.

50b). The Mishnah specifies various stages of this instruction (*m. Avot* 5:21): at age five, a child must begin studying the Torah; at the age of ten, the Mishnah; and at the age of fifteen, the Gemara. No doubt then the disciples of Jesus enjoyed this Jewish education and were, therefore, well versed in the Scriptures and well trained in theological dialectics. The picture that is sometimes drawn of the disciple of Jesus as a naive ignoramus—either to disqualify the Christian message or to justify one's spiritual and intellectual laziness—

does not fit historical reality. And if there is any doubt left on that matter, it is enough to be exposed to their writings—a clear evidence of their mature thinking and advanced theological education.

Jewish Writings

We must first of all remember that the early Christians had the same Holy Scriptures as other Jews. Significantly, when they referred to what Christians later came to call the Old Testament, they used the technical Greek word *graphai* (Luke 24:27; John 5:39; 1 Corinthians 15:3; 2 Timothy 3:16). This word, meaning "writings," was the Greek rendering of the Hebrew word *ha-ketuvim* (writings), which was used in ancient rabbinic literature as a designation for the Holy Scriptures (*m. Yadayim* 3:5). The longer whole expression *kitvey ha-qodesh* (holy writings) was also fairly common in tannaitic sources (*m. Shabbat* 16:1; *m. Yadayim* 3:2; *m. Parah* 10:3). The Greek words for "holy writings" *(hierai graphai)* or simply for "writings" *(graphai)* were also current in Jewish Hellenistic circles (Philo, *On Flight and Finding* 1:4; *Letter of Aristeas* 155, 168).

It is important to notice that when Christians began to receive additional writings, they never intended to set them up as a separate entity to replace the other Holy Scriptures. The "Christian" Scriptures were simply added to the Scriptures, or rather they were included in them. In his second letter, Peter, speaking about Paul's writings, says that they have been twisted by some "as they do the other scriptures" (2 Peter 3:16). These "new" writings were then designated by the same word: *graphai*. And, indeed, a close observation of these writings confirms this relationship.

The Two Writings

The relationship between the new Christian writings and the Jewish Scriptures is already clear on a historical level. Indeed, the New Testament situates itself as a mere continuation of the Old Testament. Speaking to his contemporary Jews, the author of the Epistle to the Hebrews emphasized this very point: "Long ago God spoke to our ancestors in many and various ways by the prophets, but in these last days he has spoken to us by a Son, whom he appointed heir of all things, through whom he also created the worlds" (Hebrews 1:1–2). It is the same God, the God of Israel, who is recognized and confessed in the New Testament: on the birth of John the Baptist, Zechariah, his father, praised this God: "Blessed be the Lord God of Israel, / for he has looked favorably on his people and redeemed them" (Luke 1:68); when Jesus performed miracles "the crowd was amazed. . . . And they praised the God of Israel" (Matthew 15:31); for Paul, addressing the people of Jerusalem in the synagogue, "the God of this people Israel" who "chose our ancestors" was the very same God who "brought to Israel a Savior, Jesus" (Acts 13:17, 23).

In fact, most if not all of the theological themes of the Old Testament recur in the New Testament. Old Testament scholar Gerhard von Rad enumerates some of them on the basis of Romans 9:4–5: sonship, glory of God, making covenants, giving of the law, worship, promises, patriarchs, Messiah.[22]

New Testament faith *(pistis)* is of the same nature as Old Testament faith. It implies the same belief in the supernatural events recorded in the Old Testament, such as creation, the flood, the miraculous birth of Isaac, the exodus, the fall of Jericho, and the same hope in the future deliverance. It is significant that this

---

[22] Gerhard von Rad, *Old Testament Theology* (trans. D. M. G. Stalker; 2 vols.; New York: Harper & Row, 1962), 2:337.

"Christian" faith is illustrated by people taken from the ancient history of Israel: Abraham, Isaac, Jacob, Joseph, Moses, Rahab, Gideon, Daniel, etc. (Hebrews 11). Even

The overall structure of the New Testament is modeled on the Old Testament Scriptures.

further, the authors of the New Testament not only think of the Old Testament and refer to it—they quote it. In the Greek New Testament, three hundred verses of the Old Testament are explicitly quoted. Many words of the New Testament, although Greek words, in fact convey Hebrew meanings. This observation is important, for it warns us against any mechanical understanding of New Testament discourse through mere reference to its Classical Greek or contemporary Hellenistic environment. The New Testament writers spoke and wrote in Greek, but they thought in Hebrew. When, for instance, the Greek word *psyche* (soul) is used, it does not mean "soul" in the Classical Greek sense, as a spiritual entity distinct from the body. It is used with the Old Testament meaning: that is, as the seat of the will, desires, and affections (Matthew 26:38; Mark 12:30; 14:34; Luke 1:46) or as a paraphrase for person or self (Matthew 11:29; Mark 8:36; Acts 2:41; Romans 2:9).

Even the overall structure of the New Testament is modeled on the Old Testament Scriptures. Thus the order of the books in the New Testament shows some parallels with that of the Hebrew Scriptures (*Tanakh*[23]):

Tanakh	New Testament
I. The foundational books (Torah)[24]	I. The foundational books (Gospels)
II. The Prophets Early prophets Prophetic literature	II. Prophetic writings Early proclamation (Acts) Prophetic literature (Epistles)
III. Writings Daniel	III. Apocalypse

[23] *Tanakh,* an acronym, combines the first letters of the three divisions of the Hebrew Bible: *Torah* (Law), *Nevi'im* (Prophets), and *Ketuvim* (Writings).

[24] The word Torah derives from *yarah,* "to teach, to instruct." The Torah refers to the five books of Moses, or to the Ten Commandments (Deca-

Moreover, the two Testaments begin and end the same way. The book of Matthew, the first book of the New Testament, starts with a genealogy; likewise, the book of Genesis, the first book of the Old Testament, starts with a genealogy, since the creation story is written in the literary form of a genealogy.[25] The first words of Matthew's genealogy *(geneseōs)* contain a deliberate allusion to the formula used in Genesis 2:4, which designates the literary genre of the creation story. The Hebrew word underlying Greek *geneseōs* in Matthew 1:1 is *toledoth* (genealogy), as attested in the Septuagint version of Genesis, where the Greek word *geneseōs* translates the Hebrew word *toledoth*.

Moreover, the Gospels of Mark and John begin on a note reflecting Genesis 1. Both (Mark 1:1; John 1:1) use the technical word *archē* (beginnings), which is the Greek translation of the Hebrew word *bereshith* (beginnings) in Genesis 1:1. John goes even further; he develops his prologue on the literary model of the creation story in Genesis.[26]

The Gospel of Luke seems to be an exception, since it starts instead with a reference to the contemporary situation, in the style typical of Hellenistic literary prologues.[27] But it is significant that as soon as the author of the gospel situates Jesus in history, he includes a genealogy that takes us back directly to creation (Luke 3:38).

The last book of the New Testament, the book of Revelation, concludes with hope in the expectation of the second coming and the

logue), or to the whole Old Testament revelation *(Torah she-bi-khetav:* Written Torah). In Judaism however, Torah will take on a still broader meaning, including also the oral traditions and interpretations, such as the Talmud and the Mishnah *(Torah she-be-al-peh:* Oral Torah).

[25] See Claus Westermann, "Genesis," *Interpreter's Dictionary of the Bible, Supplementary Volume* (ed. Keith R. Crim; Nashville: Abingdon, 1976), 358; Jacques B. Doukhan, *The Genesis Creation Story: Its Literary Structure* (Andrews University Seminary Dissertation Series 5; Berrien Springs, Mich.: Andrews University Press, 1978), 167–82.

[26] Leon Morris, *The Gospel according to John* (Grand Rapids: Eerdmans, 1971), 72–87.

[27] See H. J. Cadbury, "Commentary on the Preface of Luke," in *The Beginnings of Christianity* (ed. F. J. Foakes-Jackson and Kirsopp Lake; 5 vols.; London: Macmillan, 1920), 2:490; V. K. Robbins, "Prefaces in Greco-Roman Biography and Luke–Acts," *Perspectives in Religious Studies* 6 (1979): 94–108.

perspective of the promised land and the new Jerusalem (Revelation 21–22). Likewise, the Second Book of Chronicles, which concludes the Old Testament in the Jewish Bible, ends with hope in the expectation of the coming of Cyrus and the perspective of the new Jerusalem (2 Chronicles 36:23). It is also noteworthy that the book of Malachi, which concludes the Old Testament in the Christian Bible, following the order of the Vulgate (without the Apocrypha), ends in the same manner with a note of hope, in the expectation of the Day of the Lord (Malachi 4).

The "New" Testament was written by Jews and most of it was originally intended for Jews. It is as Jewish a book as the "Old" Testament and other traditional Jewish writings like the Talmud and Mishnah.

The "New" Testament was written by Jews and most of it was originally intended for Jews. It is as Jewish a book as the "Old" Testament and other traditional Jewish writings like the Talmud and Mishnah.

Jewish Teaching

Although Jesus, Paul, and all early Christians were Jewish, their theology is sometimes treated as if they were not Jews. It may, therefore, surprise or shock some to learn that the teaching of the early Christians, the teaching of Jesus, the teaching of Paul (the first "Christian" theologian), and ultimately the teaching of the whole New Testament was Jewish in essence.

The teaching of Jesus is clear on that matter. To the multitudes and to his disciples he affirmed and recommended faithfulness to Jewish traditions; he even acknowledged the authority of the rabbis of his time: "The scribes and the Pharisees sit on Moses' seat; therefore, do whatever they teach you and follow it" (Matthew 23:2–3). When Jesus explained that he came not "to abolish the law or the prophets . . . but to fulfill" (Matthew 5:17), he did not mean to weaken the value of the law, that is, to say that the law was no longer valid. The Greek word *plēroō* translated here by "fulfill" means "to make complete." As attested in the Greek Septuagint, behind this Greek work is the Hebrew word *ml'*, which means "to fill, to make full, to bring to plenitude." This meaning does not imply that the law is finished. In fact, Jesus then warns against this thinking:

> For truly I tell you, until heaven and earth pass away, not one letter, not one stroke of a letter, will pass from the law until all is accomplished. Therefore, whoever breaks one of the least of these commandments, and teaches others to do the same, will be called least in the kingdom of heaven; but whoever does them and teaches them will be called great in the kingdom of heaven. For I tell you, unless your righteousness exceeds that of the scribes and Pharisees, you will never enter the kingdom of heaven. (Matthew 5:18–20)

From this passage, New Testament scholar David Holwerda concludes unambiguously: "Therefore, according to Jesus, the law retains its validity in the Christian era and retains it as a whole and in all of its parts. That is, of no part of the law can it simply be said, 'This is rescinded, this is cancelled.' "[28] The conclusion of Jesus (Matthew 5:20) even suggests that obedience to the law goes deeper. Jesus is more demanding than "the scribes and Pharisees." Mechanical obedience is not enough; obedience should be complete, from the heart. And, indeed, in the following verses, Jesus takes up the practical application of this attitude:

> You have heard that it was said to those of ancient times, "You shall not murder"; and "whoever murders shall be liable to judgment." But I say to you that if you are angry with a brother or sister, you will be liable to judgment; and if you insult a brother or sister, you will be liable to the council; and if you say, "You fool," you will be liable to the hell of fire. . . . You have heard that it was said, "You shall not commit adultery." But I say to you that everyone who looks at a woman with lust has already committed adultery with her in his heart. (Matthew 5:21–22, 27–28)

The law written in people's hearts becomes much more demanding than the law written in stone. For when the law is in the heart, the whole person is involved, including the most intimate motivations.

---

[28] David E. Holwerda, *Jesus and Israel: One Covenant or Two?* (Grand Rapids: Eerdmans, 1995), 132.

And even when Jesus seems to challenge the authority of the scribes when he contrasts "you have heard" with "I say," he is in fact supporting and exalting the law, for the context of the second element does not contradict the ideal contained in the first. "On the contrary," says Jewish scholar David Daube, "wider and deeper though it may be, it is thought of as, in a sense, resulting from and certainly including the old rule, it is the revelation of a fuller meaning for a new age. The second member unfolds rather than sweeps away the first."[29]

The same faithfulness to the law is defended in Paul's writings. As Mark Nanos observes, Paul did not "believe that his gospel opposed Torah."[30] In fact, far from teaching the devaluation of the law, Paul demonstrated instead its vital necessity; for Paul, the law remains all the more precious: "I delight in the law of God" (Romans 7:22).

Furthermore, according to Paul, disobedience to the law, which he equates with sin (Romans 4:15), is much less justifiable from the perspective of grace. The difference is that now submission and obedience arise "from the heart" (Romans 6:17).

However, this spiritual revolution can take place only from the experience of a special relationship with God, when obedience is lived not with the mentality of a mercenary, but with the mentality of a child (see Romans 8:15–17). The mercenary obeys in order to get something, while the child obeys because he or she already has it. For the mercenary, the law is merely external, like rules or policies that all must accept. For the child, the law is within the heart; it causes obedience and service not because of obligation, but as a loving response to God's love. Incidentally, the same concept is advocated by the ancient rabbis. Already in the second century B.C.E., we learn that Antigonus of Socho taught that "we should not be like servants who serve the master for the sake of receiving a reward" (m. Avot 1:3).[31]

---

[29] David Daube, The New Testament and Rabbinic Judaism (New York: Arno, 1973), 60.

[30] Mark D. Nanos, The Mystery of Romans: The Jewish Context of Paul's Letter (Minneapolis: Fortress, 1996), 176.

[31] Quotations from the Mishnah are taken from The Mishnah (trans. Herbert Danby; Oxford: Oxford University Press, 1933).

The experience of grace and Christian faith is therefore not opposed to the law; on the contrary, it implies it and even upholds it. As the Apostle Paul puts it: "Do we then overthrow the law by this faith? By no means! On the contrary, we uphold the law" (Romans 3:31).

Even the "Christian" idea of grace was not a new concept in Jewish thinking. It was well attested in the Old Testament Scriptures and rendered linguistically through a variety of Hebrew words: *hen* (the idea of gift; Genesis 33:15), and *hesed* (the idea of kindness and strength; Genesis 39:21; 47:29; Esther 2:9; Proverbs 3:3). Both these words are translated in the Septuagint by the technical Greek word for grace, *charis.* Grace is also seen in biblical events such as creation and the exodus, and paradoxically, in wars (i e , God's grace

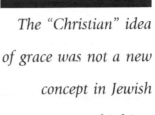

The "Christian" idea of grace was not a new concept in Jewish thinking.

is operating for the benefit of the victors). Furthermore, grace was related to law. It is the experience of grace that led to submission to the law (Exodus 19:4–5; Psalm 119:41–45). The Torah was given as an expression of God's grace and love (Deuteronomy 7:8–9). The law was even identified with grace and received as a gift from God (Exodus 24:12; Nehemiah 9:12); it is explicitly identified as a gift of grace (Psalm 119:29) In rabbinic Judaism, the life of Torah does not exclude the recognition of grace; there also grace and law go together in tension, as attested in Akiba's famous dictum: "The world is judged by grace, yet all is according to the amount of work" (*m. Avot* 3:16).

The New Covenant

The "old" law, the Jewish Torah, is then still valid under the Christian economy. But there is more. Even this ideal of internalization of the law is not new. Indeed, many passages of the Old Testament sing the love of the law: "Oh, how I love your law! It is my meditation all day long" (Psalm 119:97; cf. vv. 48, 113). From the old Shema recorded in Deuteronomy 6, the Jew constantly remembered the importance of love and of the heart in relation to the commandments: "Hear, O Israel: The LORD is our God, the LORD alone. You shall love the LORD your God with all your heart, and with all your soul, and with all your might. Keep these words that I am commanding you today in your heart" (Deuteronomy 6:4–6). It is certainly this text that is in the background of Jeremiah 31:31–33 when the prophet urges his people to refresh their relationship with God:

> The days are surely coming, says the LORD, when I will make a new covenant with the house of Israel and the house of Judah. It will not be like the covenant that I made with their ancestors when I took them by the hand to bring them out of the land of Egypt—a covenant that they broke, though I was their husband, says the LORD. But this is the covenant that I will make with the house of Israel after those days, says the LORD: I will put my law within them, and I will write it on their hearts; and I will be their God, and they shall be my people.

That this passage from the prophet Jeremiah is literally quoted in the Epistle to the Hebrews to qualify the Christian experience is significant of the intention of the New Testament writer not to break from the ancient law. For the passage of Jeremiah says just the contrary. The "new covenant," indeed, means that God will put his law "within them, and . . . will write it on their hearts" (Jeremiah 31:33). The words "I will write it" point to the Decalogue, the only document ever written by God (Exodus 34:1). Then follows the technical formula used in the Old Testament to express the confirmation of the covenant: "I will be their God, and they shall be my people" (Jeremiah 31:33; cf. 30:22; 31:1).

The new covenant that Jeremiah describes, far from abolishing the law, upholds it. The new covenant is in fact a deepening, a reviving, a renewing of the old law.

We should note, however, that only the Decalogue, the Ten Commandments on stone, is implied here. The so-called ceremonial laws connected to the sacrifices were no longer valid in the new covenant as understood by the Christians. Thus, along with the interiorization of the law, which gave more force to the Decalogue, the new covenant promoted a spiritualization of the sacrificial rites, which implied their abrogation.

Under the Christian economy, sacrifices were no longer necessary, not only because they were interpreted as a "type" and a "shadow" of the Messiah (Colossians 2:17; Hebrews 8:5; 10:1), but also because they were identified with prayers and good deeds!

"Through him, then, let us continually offer a sacrifice of praise to God, that is, the fruit of lips that confess his name. Do not neglect to do good and to share what you have, for such sacrifices are pleasing to God" (Hebrews 13:15–16).

It is noteworthy that this typological and ethical interpretation of the sacrifices is paralleled in the Bible and in Jewish tradition. Already the prophets of the First Temple period often emphasized the value of the spiritual and ethical lessons of the sacrifices at the expense of the ritual per se (Amos 5:16; Micah 6:8; see also Psalms 40:6–8; 50:8–15; Proverbs 15:8; 21:3, 27). This move became more prominent in the course of the Babylonian exile and the Diaspora and under the influence of Jewish philosophers such as Philo.[32] In fact, a good portion of the orthodox Judaism contemporaneous with early Christianity, represented especially by the Pharisees and the Essenes, argued on behalf of the transient nature and forcefully pled for a spiritualization of the sacrificial rites.[33] This connection with sacrificial rites is attested in rabbinic literature: "In the name of R. Jose b. Hanina, R. Joseph queried: [Do we need] to fix a *halachah* for [the days of] the Messiah?—Abaye answered: If so, we should not study the laws of sacrifices, as they are also only for the Messianic era."[34] The ethical application of the sacrifices was taught as well: "What can be substituted for the oxen which we used to offer unto Thee? Our lips, with the prayer which we offer unto Thee" (*Pesiqta de Rab Kahana* 24:19 [English translation by Brande and Kapstein]; cf. Hebrews 13:15).

The Apostolic Decree

To argue from the apostolic decree, recorded in Acts 15, that Paul ultimately compromised and rejected the law for the sake of the

---

[32] *Philo, with an English Translation*, by F. H. Colson (The Loeb Classical Library; Cambridge, Mass.: Harvard, 1937), 7:195–256.

[33] Only the priests and the Sadducees were defending the sacrifices, because their economical and political interests depended on them. But considering their involvement with the occupying power and their social abuses, they remained a despised minority with no credibility in the Jewish Palestinian society on matters of religious and spiritual authority.

[34] *B. Sanhedrin* 51b; English translation in I. Epstein, ed., *The Babylonian Talmud* (London: Soncino, 1935), 346; cf. *b. Zevahim* 44b.

Gentiles is to ignore Paul's intention and the specific Jewish setting of the Jerusalem Council. It is interesting to note that the only law questioned here is circumcision. The discussion never touched on the Sabbath or even the food laws. The reason for this distinction is not arbitrary, for Jewish tradition knew two types of laws: the Torah, which bound only the Jew, and the so-called Noachide laws, which bound also the Gentile. Although the principle of two sets of laws is not formally spelled out in the Bible, it contains both the Mosaic prescriptions to the Jews and also a set of laws incumbent upon "the stranger within your gates." Like the apostolic decree (Acts 15:20–21, 28–29), these laws included the forbiddance of (1) idolatry (Leviticus 17:7–9), (2) eating blood and unclean meat (Leviticus 17:13–14), (3) work on the Sabbath[35] (Exodus 20:10), and (4) sexual immorality (Leviticus 18:6–26). It is most likely, then, that the apostolic decree reflects a step in the development of the tradition of the Noachide commandments, which take final shape only later in the talmudic period (250–500 C.E.; *b. Sanhedrin* 56a; *b. Hullin* 92a). That circumcision was not imposed on Gentiles who wanted to join the Christian faith does not imply the intention to abrogate the law as a whole. Jewish theologian Michael Wyschogrod explains the controversy of Acts 15 along these lines: "It is quite clear . . . that both factions in Jerusalem agreed that Jews, even after Jesus, remained under the prescriptions of the Torah. If the Jesus event had changed Jewish Torah obligation, then it would hardly make any sense to argue whether non-Jews required circumcision and Torah obligation. The debate concerned Gentiles; both sides agreed about the Torah obligation of Jesus-believing Jews."[36]

---

[35] In the report of the apostolic decree the keeping of the Sabbath is implied in Acts 15:21. See also Isaiah 56:6, which presents the Sabbath as "an essential mark of acceptability for the would-be proselyte"; James D. G. Dunn, *The Partings of the Ways: Between Christianity and Judaism and Their Significance for the Character of Christianity* (London: SCM/Philadelphia: Trinity, 1991), 30.

[36] Michael Wyschogrod, "A Jewish View of Christianity," in *Toward a Theological Encounter: Jewish Understandings of Christianity* (ed. Leon Klenicki; Mahwah, N.J.: Paulist, 1991), 119.

It is significant indeed that the same tolerance was practiced within orthodox Judaism. And in Judaism as well as in early Christianity, Gentiles who converted were subject to the law anyway. As New Testament scholar Jacob Jervell puts it: "Luke knows of no Gentile mission that is free from the law. He knows about a Gentile mission without circumcision, not without the law. The apostolic decree enjoins Gentiles to keep the law, and they keep that part of the law required for them to live together with Jews."[37]

Indeed, early Christians were Jews, not only ethnically or legally because they were of Jewish lineage, not only culturally or religiously because they practiced Judaism and observed faithfully the Jewish law, but also theologically because they professed and taught traditional Jewish values and truths.

Even when Jesus or Paul or any New Testament writer seems to imply something new, it does not mean that it was never taught before in the Old Testament or was absent in contemporary Judaism. It was new in the sense that the "old" truth always required a fresh rediscovery, a new commitment. When Jesus says, for instance, to his disciples, "I give you a new commandment, that you love one another. Just as I have loved you, you also should love one another" (John 13:34), he did not in fact give a *new* commandment, for the commandment of love was already given through Moses: "You shall love your neighbor as yourself: I am the LORD" (Leviticus 19:18). And in both cases, human love is enrooted in and inspired by one's relationship with the Lord.

Even the new elements—the coming of the Messiah, the proclamation of the kingdom of God, and fulfillments of the old promises—are not new revelation that makes the old revelation obsolete. Already, Israel of old knew the experience of fulfillments. The event of the exodus and the conquest of Canaan was given as a fulfillment of the old promises to the patriarchs (Exodus 3:7–8; 6:2–4; Genesis 12:7; 15:18). The return from Babylonian exile was also received as a fulfillment of the prophetic word (Ezra 7:27–28; Daniel 9:2; Jeremiah 25:11; 2 Chronicles 36:21). These fulfillments never implied the rejection of the Torah; on the contrary, they brought

---

[37] Jacob Jervell, *Luke and the People of God: A New Look at Luke–Acts* (Minneapolis: Augsburg, 1972), 144.

along a new urge to walk on "the ancient paths" (Jeremiah 6:16). Likewise, in the New Testament, the encounter with the Messiah and the experience of a new relationship with the Lord did not mean the abandonment of Jewish roots. Early Christians were Jews. They never considered themselves as "converted Jews." Neither Jesus nor Paul "converted" to Christianity, for at that time there was no such a thing as a Christian church. Significantly, when Paul speaks of the ideal believer, he does not define himself as the true Christian, but instead as "the true Jew" (Romans 2:28–29). The "Christian" religion was not for them a new religion, or even a "form of Judaism"; it was Judaism in its truest sense. In fact, because they were Jews, they embraced the "Christian faith," which they felt was in essence the Jewish faith.[38]

Early Christians were Jews. They never considered themselves as "converted Jews."

WHEN JEWS WERE CHRISTIANS

We are all willing to recognize that the early Christians were Jews. The above demonstration was just a reminder of what many know and easily assume today. Yet, there is a much more disturbing truth for many Christians, which Jews have not yet fully realized and are hardly ready to welcome; it concerns the importance of the Christian impact on the Jewish community in the early centuries.

Christians have traditionally described Jews as those who rejected and crucified Jesus. For New Testament scholar David Holwerda, "the rejection of Jesus by unbelieving Israel" makes it evident that "most of Israel remained unconvinced and unbelieving."[39] Judaism has likewise defined itself on this rejection. Modern Judaic scholar David Novak states: "The normative Jewish community decided in the first century that Jesus of Nazareth was not the

---

[38] Holwerda, *Jesus and Israel*, 29.
[39] Ibid., 54.

Messiah."[40] But a close look at the ancient writings describing these early stages of Christian history reveal another picture altogether. From the beginning to the end of his public life and beyond, Jesus was indeed welcomed and followed by a majority of Jews.

The Jews of Jesus

Wherever Jesus went in Palestine, whether in Galilee or Judea, he met with the same enthusiastic and popular response: "Then Jesus, filled with the power of the Spirit, returned to Galilee, and a report about him spread through all the surrounding country. He began to teach in their synagogues and was praised by everyone" (Luke 4:14–15). "He left that place and went to the region of Judea and beyond the Jordan. And crowds again gathered around him; and, as was his custom, he again taught them" (Mark 10:1). "All the people were spellbound by what they heared" (Luke 19:48). The popularity of Jesus in the Jewish community remained high until the end. Right before the last Passover, the book of Luke reports Jesus' popularity: "And all the people would get up early in the morning to listen to him in the temple" (Luke 21:38).

From the beginning to the end of his public life and beyond, Jesus was indeed welcomed and followed by a majority of Jews.

Jews at the Cross

Yet, Jesus was sentenced to death, traditionally pictured by Christians as a big crowd of Jews shouting, "Crucify him!" How can we explain this sudden shift from love to hatred? How can we reconcile the great popularity of Jesus for so many years and the admiration of the majority of the Jews with this one-day change and this demand for the death sentence? Political opportunism or fickle

---

[40] David Novak, "Why Judaism and Jesus Don't Mix," *Moment* (August 1994): 34.

human changeableness could be a part of the answer. But even if we take these factors into consideration, we still stumble on the testimony of the New Testament, which clearly and unambiguously repeats that only a small minority of Jews were involved. And these few men were in fact worried precisely because they were observing that a growing majority of Jewish people was responding positively to Jesus. Each gospel reports this minority viewpoint.

Matthew: "When the chief priests and the Pharisees heard his parables, they realized that he was speaking about them. They wanted to arrest him, but they feared the crowds, because they regarded him as a prophet" (Matthew 21:45–46). "Then the chief priests and the elders of the people gathered in the palace of the high priest, who was called Caiaphas, and they conspired to arrest Jesus by stealth and kill him. But they said, 'Not during the festival, or there may be a riot among the people' " (Matthew 26:3–5).

Mark: "When they realized that he had told this parable against them, they wanted to arrest him, but they feared the crowd. So they left him and went away" (Mark 12:12). "It was two days before the Passover and the festival of Unleavened Bread. The chief priests and the scribes were looking for a way to arrest Jesus by stealth and kill him; for they said, 'Not during the festival, or there may be a riot among the people' " (Mark 14:1–2).

Luke: "Every day he was teaching in the temple. The chief priests, the scribes, and the leaders of the people kept looking for a way to kill him; but they did not find anything they could do, for all the people were spellbound by what they heard" (Luke 19:47–48). "The chief priests and the scribes were looking for a way to put Jesus to death, for they were afraid of the people" (Luke 22:2).

John: "Many of the Jews therefore, who had come with Mary and had seen what Jesus did, believed in him. But some of them went to the Pharisees and told them what he had done. So the chief priests and the Pharisees called a meeting of the council, and said, 'What are we to do? This man is performing many signs. If we let him go on like this, everyone will believe in him, and the Romans will come and destroy both our holy place and our nation.' But one of them, Caiaphas, who was high priest that year, said to them, 'You know nothing at all! You do not understand that it is better for you to have one man die for the people than to have the whole nation destroyed' " (John 11:45–50).

The Gospels thus tell a story that squarely contradicts the traditional Jewish-Christian belief that the majority of Jews rejected Jesus and supported his execution. Quite to the contrary, because the majority of the Jews was behind Jesus and because, if we believe Caiaphas, the majority could become "the whole nation," a small group of leaders was concerned and decided to kill Jesus. It is also because the majority of the Jews was behind Jesus that, for fear of scandal and tumult (Luke 23:14; cf. Mark 14:2), these leaders deliberately chose to bring Jesus to judgment during the night (Matthew 26:31; 27:1). This procedure was highly irregular. Indeed, the Talmud prescribes that no trial, and especially not a trial involving an alleged capital offense, should be conducted on the eve of the Sabbath or a festival (*m. Sanhedrin* 4:1). Likewise, they ignored the mishnaic principle that trials in which human life is at stake must take place in the light of the day (*m. Sanhedrin* 4:1). But who, then, would have made up the throng that crowded into the praetorium?

A minority of Palestinian Jews. To be sure, in the ranks of that motley crowd were some who had known Jesus—some who had been touched by his message. But people forget easily or, like Peter, they prefer to remain silent or, like Judas, they allow themselves to be carried along with the crowd, to the point that events finally take over completely, leading them into unanticipated trouble.

Some priests. Indeed, the priests led out in this whole matter. They arrested Jesus and incited the people to shout, "Crucify him!" (Mark 15:13). It was also the priests who answered Pilate with the words "we have no king but the emperor" (John 19:15), a statement that very well fits the historical data, for the priests felt a greater degree of solidarity with the Roman power than with the common people. Nominated by the Roman governor, they were, in fact, captive to him. They were stringently dependent on the Roman procurator, who kept custody, under lock and key, of their priestly garments and ornaments (Josephus, *Jewish Antiquities* 20.6–7).

No wonder then that the Palestinian Jews, who witnessed these conditions on a daily basis, despised the priests and considered them traitors in the employ of Rome. Flavius Josephus describes the priests as using "violence with the people, and were ready to plunder those that were weaker than themselves" (*Jewish Antiquities* 20.214).

A popular song recorded in the Talmud preserved the feelings of the people toward the priests of that time:

> Woe is me because of the house of Boethus; woe is me because of their staves. Woe is me because of the house of Hanin; woe is me because of their whisperings. Woe is me because of the house of Kathros, woe is me because of their pens! Woe is me because of the house of Ishmael the son of Phabi, woe is me because of their fists! For they are High Priests and their sons are [Temple] treasurers and their sons-in-law are trustees and their servants beat the people with staves.[41]

Some Jews from the Diaspora. It would seem, therefore, that the crowd massed before the praetorium was made up largely of Jews unacquainted with Jesus and ignorant regarding the priests and their abuses. The crowd was most probably from abroad. Jesus' reputation had not yet spread beyond the Palestinian frontiers. No Jewish writer of the Diaspora mentions Jesus during that period. Philo of Alexandria, for instance, who was contemporary to Jesus, mentions Pilate but says not a word about the Galilean teacher.

Let's not forget that the crucifixion took place at Passover—a time when many Jews of the Diaspora were in the country. People from the four corners of the earth camped all around Jerusalem. They pressed in close to the city because the Passover lamb could be sacrificed only in the temple (see Deuteronomy 12:13–14, 26; 16:2). The Diaspora had been a historical fact for eight centuries, and the majority of the Jewish people no longer lived in Palestine.[42]

At the time of the crucifixion, therefore, one could find, in the streets of Jerusalem, Jews from all parts of the world (Acts 2:9–11). In other words, Jews that knew Jesus and Jews that had never before heard of him. The New Testament account alludes to these two categories of Israelites: "When he [Jesus] entered Jerusalem, the

---

[41] *Pesahim* 57a, English translation by I. Epstein, *The Babylonian Talmud* (London: Soncino Press, 1938), *Seder Mo'ed*, 285.

[42] Jules Isaac, *Jesus and Israel* (ed. Claire H. Bishop; trans. Sally Gran; New York: Holt, Rinehart & Winston, 1971), 93.

whole city was in turmoil, asking, 'Who is this?' The crowds were saying, 'This is the prophet Jesus from Nazareth in Galilee' " (Matthew 21:10–11).

Could it not be that we have here a key to the problem—an explanation of the contradiction we encountered earlier? The crowd that condemned Jesus could have been composed chiefly of Diaspora Jews who were ignorant concerning both Jesus and the priests and who, therefore, were easy prey for the manipulating priests.

Under the urging of the priests, the clamor broke forth. Perhaps a minority of Palestinian Jews had allowed themselves, by weakness, by lack of forethought and understanding, to be carried along to deny the one they had loved and acclaimed; while others, perhaps the majority, had followed the same course without really knowing anything about the one they voted to crucify.

What is interesting is that Jesus himself on the cross testifies to the same view. Knowing the situation, Jesus prays, "Father, forgive them; for they do not know what they are doing" (Luke 23:34). Too often, this final supplication is overlooked and people prefer to remember instead the fateful words of the throng: "His blood be on us and on our children" (Matthew 27:25). We may wonder, however, which one of the two prayers was the most worthy to be heard and answered, the prayer of the ignorant little group of people, or the prayer of the Holy One crucified? Many of those who shouted were from abroad; they did not know the situation about the priests.

And even then, the number of those Jews who shouted was insignificant. It is enough to visit the site of the praetorium where the event actually took place to realize how small was the crowd. Indeed, the praetorium would hardly take more than a hundred people, which also included a good number of Roman soldiers and officers who were present to carry out the sentence.

Some Romans. The way Jesus was mishandled, the fact that he was crucified instead of being stoned (the usual Jewish practice), the method used to bury him—all confirm once again that the whole case was conducted outside of Jewish influence. That Jewish leaders had to resort to the Romans to carry out the sentence shows the serious lack of support on the part of the Jewish population at large.

Ironically, the cross, which was later to become for Christians the sign par excellence of Jewish guilt, is in actuality the sign of Jewish innocence; it is the legal evidence, the proof, that Jesus was put to death without the backing of the majority of the Jews.

The Jews for Jesus

Even after his death, the popularity of Jesus did not decline among Jews. It seems instead that the number of Jewish disciples increased at great speed. A cursory reading of the book of Acts reveals this success story. Acts 2 reports that the gathering of Pentecost in Jerusalem ended up with the baptism of "about three thousand persons" (Acts 2:41). A few verses later, the author further comments: "And day by day the Lord added to their number those who were being saved" (Acts 2:47). Then in Acts 4 after the preaching of Peter and John in the temple (chapter 3), the text says that "many of those who heard the word believed; and they numbered about five thousand" (Acts 4:4). And this figure does not include women and children. Later, the chapter speaks about "the whole group of those who believed" (Acts 4:32; Greek *plēthos,* "great number, multitude").

Ironically, the cross, which was later to become for Christians the sign par excellence of Jewish guilt, is in actuality the sign of Jewish innocence.

We read again in chapter 5 that "a great number of people would also gather from the towns around Jerusalem, bringing the sick . . . and they were all cured" (Acts 5:16). Chapter 6 specified that "the word of God continued to spread; the number of the disciples increased greatly in Jerusalem" (Acts 6:7). Note that even "a great many of the priests became obedient to the faith" (Acts 6:7b).

The event of the stoning of Stephen did not stop the process; contrary to what many Christians may assume, the success of the Christian outreach among Jews kept growing. It was after the stoning of Stephen that Paul (Saul) accepted the Christian message (Acts 9:1–17). The same chapter says that Paul immediately started preaching

"Jesus in the synagogues," and "all who heard him were amazed" (Acts 9:20–21), and he was able to prove to the Jews who were there "that Jesus was the Messiah" (Acts 9:22). Verse 31 sums up the situation: "Meanwhile the church throughout Judea, Galilee, and Samaria had peace and was built up. . . . It increased in numbers."

Chapter 11 tells us that "those who were scattered because of the persecution that took place over Stephen traveled as far as Phoenicia, Cyprus, and Antioch, and they spoke the word to no one except Jews" (Acts 11:19), and "a great number became believers and turned to the Lord" (Acts 11:21).

In chapter 13, we learn that Paul traveled to Cyprus, where he "proclaimed the word of God in the synagogues of the Jews" (Acts 13:5; cf. v. 15); and at Antioch in Pisidia "many Jews and devout converts to Judaism followed Paul and Barnabas. . . . The next sabbath almost the whole city gathered to hear the word of the Lord" (Acts 13:43–44). Chapter 14 relates that in Iconium Paul and Barnabas again spoke in the synagogue and "a great number of both Jews and Greeks became believers" (Acts 14:1). Chapter 15 mentions that "some believers who belonged to the sect of the Pharisees" (Acts 15:5) had become members of the early Christian community.

And finally, when Paul returns to Jerusalem and reports his success in the Diaspora, James, the leader of the Jerusalem community, responds and tells about the believers in his own city: "You see, brother, how many thousands of believers there are among the Jews, and they are all zealous for the law" (Acts 21:20) The Greek word *myrias* means "ten thousands"; and because it is used here in plural, we understand that the number of Jews who believed was several times "ten thousands," that is, at least twenty thousand. Considering Jerusalem's population, which did not surpass thirty thousand inhabitants,[43] we may conclude that the great majority of the Jews of Jerusalem had recognized Jesus as their Messiah. This sounds unbelievable, so unbelievable indeed that a number of commentators think that it is either a gloss in the text or simply a

---

[43] See Joachim Jeremias, *Jerusalem in the Time of Jesus: An Investigation into Economic and Social Conditions during the New Testament Period* (trans. F. H. Cave and C. H. Cave; London: SCM Press, 1969), 84; cf. Magen Broshi, "Estimating the Population of Ancient Jerusalem," *Biblical Archaeology Review* 4.2 (June 1978): 10–15.

rhetorical overstatement. But these suggestions are unnecessary since the existence of a significant proportion of Jews in the early Jerusalem church is firmly attested. Furthermore, this great number is consistent with the progression we have noticed throughout the book of Acts. More and more Jews are joining the Christian community. At the end of the book, the curve of statistics is expected to reach its climax. Note the evolution of terminology describing the growth process:

three thousand
↓
many
↓
five thousand
↓
a great multitude
↓
a great number
↓
almost the whole city
↓
a great number
↓
many thousands

The last statistic takes place in Rome where Paul gathers "the local leaders of the Jews" (Acts 28:17), who incidentally observe that they had never received bad reports concerning him and his teaching from Jewish headquarters in Judea (Acts 28:21)—another hint of the Christian success in Jerusalem. In verse 22, the Jewish leaders expressed their desire "to hear" more about the Christian message, and when they "had set a day to meet with him, they came to him at his lodgings in great numbers," and he explained to them and persuaded them "from morning until evening . . . about Jesus both from the law of Moses and from the prophets" (Acts 28:23). Paul "lived there two whole years . . . and welcomed all who came to him" (Acts 28:30). Significantly, the book concludes on this note. Paul is still successfully preaching to the Jews "with all boldness and without hindrance" (Acts 28:31).

This success story was necessary to tell. For many people, the book of Acts is the occasion to lament Jewish resistance to the gospel. The book of Acts is the pretext or the proof text from which one elaborates the Jewish failure and boasts about the wonderful shift of God's interests from Jews to Gentiles. Yet, the book attests to something else. Although Christian preaching reaches out to Gentiles and the truth of the God of Israel is taken beyond the borders of Israel, the priority of the Christian proclamation remains the Jewish community. Paul, the apostle to the Gentiles (Galatians 1:15–16), still goes "first to the Jews" with the same passion and the same fruitful results. Indeed, the book does not disregard the oppositions and the failures—not all the Jews had welcomed the Christian

Whenever Jews were exposed to the Christian message, a great and growing majority and in some places the totality of the population responded positively.

message; but the objective report, the numbers and the facts, suggests that whenever Jews were exposed to the Christian message, a great and growing majority and in some places the totality of the population responded positively. This observation may be surprising and difficult to receive because of traditional thinking on that matter. Yet, more and more findings today confirm this assessment.

Recently, the same conclusion has been reached from various horizons—sociological, historical, and archaeological perspectives. Sociologist Rodney Stark, using statistics and exploring the arithmetic of growth, came to the revolutionary conclusion "that, contrary to the received wisdom, Jewish Christianity played a central role until much later in the rise of Christianity—that not only was it the Jews of the diaspora who provided the initial basis for church growth during the first and early second centuries, but that Jews continued as a significant source of Christian converts until at least as late as the fourth century."[44] He showed that "the mis-

---

[44] Rodney Stark, *The Rise of Christianity: A Sociologist Reconsiders History* (Princeton: Princeton University Press, 1996), 49.

sion to the Jews of the diaspora should have been a considerable long-run success" and suggested that "a very substantial conversion of the Jews actually did take place."[45]

It is interesting to notice that the same trend has been attested in Ethiopian tradition. Ephraim Isaac, an expert in both Jewish and Ethiopian literature and culture, writes, "Tradition also holds that when Christianity came to Ethiopia half of the population was Jewish and that most of them converted to Christianity."[46]

From archaeology comes more evidence of missionary success among the Jews. Eric Meyers reports that the wealth of archaeological findings in Palestine and in Italy (especially in Rome) shows that "Jewish and Christian burials, as in Rome, reflect an interdependent and closely related community of Jews and Christians in which clear marks of demarcation were blurred until the third and fourth centuries C.E."[47] This simple physical observation leads Meyers to conclude that "the followers of Jesus were largely indistinguishable from their fellow Jews. Although they professed a belief in the messiahship of Jesus . . . they apparently got along well with their fellow Jews."[48]

This close connection between and even the identification of Jews and Christians hints at Christian success among Jews. The number of Jews who were following Jesus was so important that no one would dare to question their Jewishness: it was a mass movement that involved in some places the majority if not the totality of the Jews.

---

[45] Ibid., 70.

[46] Ephraim Isaac, "Is the Ark of the Covenant in Ethiopia?" *Biblical Archeology Review* 19.4 (July/August 1993): 60–63.

[47] Eric Meyers, "Early Judaism and Christianity in the Light of Archaeology," *Biblical Archaeologist* 51.2 (June 1988): 69–79.

[48] Ibid., 69.

CHAPTER 2

THE PARTING OF THE WAYS

In the beginning, it was possible for a Jew to be a Christian without having to deny his or her Jewish roots, without having to leave his or her alma mater. As we just saw, a significant amount of biblical, archaeological, and sociological evidence suggests that until the fourth century Jews by thousands and hundreds of thousands were joining the "new" faith. And until then, Jews and Christians were living together in the same religious community. This simple historical fact stands in flat contradiction of the common belief that the "parting of the ways" had started in the first century, especially under the pressure of the Jewish wars and the promulgation of liturgical Jewish curses. This contradiction obliges us to reconsider the facts.

The Jewish-Christian separation was, indeed, a complex process. And it would be presumptuous to believe that we can reach a clear and definitive view of what actually happened. Yet, in light of the historical data, as dim as this may be, we may at least be able to reach the modest goal of tracing some of the most important factors that determined the parting of the ways. Only the identification of these factors will help us settle the problem of this contradiction and orient our interpretation in the right direction. We shall know then whether these factors are a part of an early process that took place on Jewish ground or if we have to wait until later in the fourth century to detect these factors in the Christian church. In other words, did the parting of the ways happen because Jews rejected Christians or because Christians rejected Jews?

THE JEWISH REJECTION

It is generally believed that the parting of the ways was a process that started in the first century and was essentially the result of Jewish initiative. According to this view, two main factors played a role in Jewish-Christian separation: (1) Jewish revolts against the Romans and (2) Jewish liturgical curses against the Christians.

The Jewish Revolts

From the book of Acts, it is evident that Jews persecuted Christians before the Jewish revolts. Yet, these incidents were only sporadic. The book of Acts records only two martyrdoms (Acts 6:9–8:2; 12:2). And even these acts of persecution were not the result of a formal decision by Jewish authorities. Rather, these conflicts should probably be viewed as a mere controversy between Jewish sects. It was still a family dispute. According to some scholars, this line of thinking changed, however, with the Jewish wars when Christians failed to support the nationalist movement against Rome and, instead of fighting along with their Jewish compatriots, chose to flee to Pella in Perea, which triggered the Jewish rejection. Christians were now seen as traitors and were no longer considered part of the family. This classic interpretation of the consequences of the Jewish revolts overlooks an important consideration: Christians were not the only Jews who did not participate in the wars against the Romans. Contrary to what is often believed, these belligerent movements did not receive much popular support. Bar Kokhba himself was not as popular as legend may suggest. In spite of Rabbi Akiba's praise, the *aggada* records serious suspicion on the part of sages who disliked his pride against God.[1] Disappointment after the de-

Contrary to what is often believed, these belligerent movements did not receive much popular support.

---

[1] See Shimem Amir, "Bar Kokhba," *Encyclopedia Judaica* (16 vols.; New York: Macmillan, 1971), 4:231.

feat and even during the revolt led people to change his name from Bar Kokhba, meaning "son of a star," an allusion to his messianic claim (cf. Numbers 24:17), to Bar Kozivah, meaning "son of a lie" (*b. Berakhot* 97b).

Also, one important branch of Pharisees, those who followed the great Hillel, refused to join the revolt and preferred negotiations over fighting. And this is the very reason why Judaism survived. Because these Jews chose not to take part in the revolt against the Romans, they were allowed to establish the first rabbinic school (around 80 C.E.) at Yavneh (Jamniah), where they reconstructed Jewish life around the Torah, producing the Mishnah (200 C.E.), which later became the basis for the Talmud. In so doing, they succeeded in creating a form of Judaism that could keep its identity without need of a geographic center or cultic entity. All other branches of Judaism disappeared: the Sadducees, when the destruction of the temple in 70 C.E. meant the fall of their political and economic foundations; the Essenes, when their base at Qumran was overthrown by Roman legions in 68 C.E.; and the Zealots, when Masada, their last outpost of resistance, fell in 73 C.E., and when their charismatic leader Bar Kokhba was crushed by the Roman army in 132–135 C.E.

It is interesting to note that rabbinic Judaism (the Pharisees) and Christianity (the "Nazarenes"; Acts 24:5) were the only survivors of early Judaism, precisely because they both decided not to resist Roman power since their respective values transcended the crumbling temporary institutions—rabbinic Judaism with the Torah and Christianity with the Messiah. And these two points of focus were not divisive. As I have already demonstrated, many Christians accommodated their faith in the Messiah very well with their faithfulness to the Torah. The picture of post-70 Judaism and post-70 Christianity is very complex, not only because each one offered a very broad spectrum of various trends, but because the two spectrums continued to overlap during the first centuries.

The common assumption that the parting of the ways was essentially promoted by the Jewish wars is then to be reconsidered on two accounts. First, Christians were not the only Jews who failed to support the Jewish revolts; along with them, many Jews, especially the Pharisees, refused to engage in the revolts against the Romans.

Second, history shows that Jews and Christians remained together even after the revolts, at least until the fourth century.

Jewish Curses

The view that the process of separation started within the synagogue has also been defended on the basis of New Testament, Jewish, and patristic evidence. It seems, indeed, that the synagogue promulgated curses and excommunication formulas against Jewish Christians and thus triggered the process of separation. Close examination of the evidence, however, suggests a more nuanced position. First of all, in the New Testament, only a few passages in the Gospel of John (9:22; 12:42; 16:2) speak about expulsion from a local assembly or building and do not in any way imply the more drastic excommunication from the Jewish community at large. In fact, there is no mention in the New Testament of any kind of Jewish excommunication formula against Christians. Besides, that Jewish Christians were free to attend synagogue, as attested in the book of Acts, is clear evidence that Christians never suffered excommunication in the full sense. Any reference to these Johannine texts as evidence of Jewish exclusionary curses against Christians is therefore unjustified.

In the discussion of the separation of church and synagogue, scholars have attributed various degrees of importance to the so-called *birkat-ha-minim*. This benediction, or rather malediction, against heretics was found in the Cairo Genizah and refers explicitly to Christians: "Let the Christians *(notzrim)* and the heretics *(minim)* perish in a moment, let them be blotted out of the book of life and let them not be written with the righteous. Blessed art thou, O Lord, who humblest the insolent."[2] This curse is a part of the twelfth benediction of the daily prayer *Shemoneh Esreh* (Eighteen Benedictions) and is believed to have been pronounced three times a day (*m. Berakhot* 3:3; 4:1). Since the discovery of this text at the end of the nineteenth century, scholars have placed great emphasis

---

[2]Translation from William Horbury, "The Benediction of the *Minim* and Early Jewish-Christian Controversy," *Journal of Theological Studies* 33 (1982): 20.

on this benediction by arguing that it was intended to be a liturgical instrument to drive Jewish Christians out of the synagogue.[3] Recent scholarship, however, has challenged this widespread opinion and established on the basis of semantic, stylistic, and historical evidence that this curse was of pre-Christian origin (probably Maccabean).[4] There are good reasons to think the word "Christians" *(notzrim)* was later added to the word "heretics" *(minim)*, around the third or fourth century as Christians became increasingly removed from Judaism and eventually became "a separate and powerfully distinct challenge to Judaism."[5] To begin with, this is the only Jewish source that explicitly mentions the *notzrim*. In all other versions, whether from Christian or non-Christian countries, where no censorship would have been expected, only the word *minim* (heretics) appears. If the text had been written in the first or second century, the word *minim*, which covers all Jewish heretic groups, would have been sufficient to include Jewish-Christians. That the word *notzrim* has been added to *minim* is clear evidence that the benediction was composed when Christians were no longer known simply as *minim*, as Jewish heretics; Christianity had become a separate entity, and Jewish-Christians had ceased to be a significant presence in the church.

Even the testimony of the church fathers confirms this conclusion. During the second and third centuries, there are no clear references to the *birkat-ha-minim* in Christian sources. Only a few

---

[3] See Adolf von Harnack, *The Expansion of Christianity in the First Three Centuries* (trans. and ed. James Moffatt; 2 vols.; London: Williams & Norgate/New York: Putnam, 1904), 1:73–83; W. H. C. Frend, *Martyrdom and Persecution in the Early Church: A Study of a Conflict from the Maccabees to Donatus* (Oxford: Blackwell, 1965), 147.

[4] Note especially David Flusser, "The Jewish Christian Schism (Part II)," *Immanuel* 17 (Winter 1983–84): 32–38; Reuven Kimelman, "*Birkat ha-Minim* and the Lack of Evidence for an Anti-Christian Jewish Prayer in Late Antiquity," in *Jewish and Christian Self-Definition: Aspects of Judaism in the Graeco-Roman Period* (ed. E. P. Sanders, A. I. Baumgarten, and Alan Mendelsohn; 2 vols.; London: SCM, 1981), 2:226–44.

[5] Steven T. Katz, "Issues in the Separation of Judaism and Christianity after 70 C.E.: A Reconsideration," *Journal of Biblical Literature* 103 (1984): 44–76; Horbury, "Benediction of the *Minim*," 19–41; Marvin R. Wilson, *Our Father Abraham: Jewish Roots of the Christian Faith* (Grand Rapids: Eerdmans, 1989), 65–70.

passages in Justin Martyr (second century) speak of Jews cursing Christians, but these curses did not involve the regular utterance of a liturgical benediction and may well have been pronounced only "informally and spasmodically."[6]

The first and perhaps only explicit mention of this liturgical benediction before the Middle Ages is found in Jerome's writings, late in the fourth century, and even this testimony is suspect, considering his well-known anti-Jewish bias and the lack of action by imperial authorities against Jews because of this account. It is also significant that Christian writers in the following centuries never accuse Jews of this cursing practice. Indeed, we have to wait until the ninth century, until Archbishop Agobard, to find a clear Christian reference to the daily Jewish practice of cursing Christians under the word *notzrim*. It is noteworthy that in the course of time, as Christian hostility grew toward Jews, this Jewish curse was given more weight than it really deserved. Significantly, this text became a linchpin in the anti-Semitic argument[7] to blame the Jews for having initiated the Jewish-Christian schism. Yet, the scanty evidence suggests that even when we find evidence of Jews using this curse, it was far from being a universal practice. Also, it was not used before the fourth or the fifth century, if we believe Jerome, or the ninth century, if we believe Agobard, thus confirming the testimony of the Cairo Synagogue, which was built in the ninth century. But it may well be that Agobard was only conjecturing on unfounded rumors. Whatever the case, it is at least clear that the curse did not have a significant impact on the process of separation since it appears only after the

> It is . . . improper to argue that the Jewish curse, or any other type of Jewish means of excommunication, triggered the Jewish-Christian separation.

---

[6] T. C. G. Thornton, "Christian Understanding of the *Birkath ha-Minim* in the Eastern Roman Empire," *Journal of Theological Studies* 38 (1987): 429.

[7] See, for instance, von Harnack, *Expansion of Christianity*, 1:73–83.

fact. It is, therefore, improper to argue that the Jewish curse, or any other type of Jewish means of excommunication, triggered the Jewish-Christian separation. Reuven Kimelman is right when he concludes his extensive treatment of the subject that "there never was a single edict which caused the so-called irreparable separation between Judaism and Christianity."[8]

And the fact that this curse is not attested before the fourth century indicates that until then being Jewish was not incompatible with being Christian. It is, for instance, of great significance that one of the most famous heretics of the Talmud, Elisha ben Abuyah, who was suspected of reading heretical books and was probably a Christian, was never subjected to any measure of excommunication. Instead, the talmudic evidence indicates continued and even respectful relations between Elisha and the sages. The same case can be made for Simeon ben Zoma, a leading second-century rabbi who was likely a believing Christian.[9] That Zoma was tolerated and treated as a leader and sage in Israel shows the kind of tolerance displayed by the rabbis and confirms that at an earlier age it was not yet a crime for a Jew to profess Jesus as Messiah. This somewhat surprising situation again confirms the conclusion that one must be skeptical concerning the existence of any form of ban against Jewish-Christians during the first three centuries.

THE CHRISTIAN REJECTION

The historical fact that Jewish-Christians were still considered full members of the Jewish community until at least the fourth century, and the absence of any substantial evidence of Jewish rejection of Christians, suggests that the decisive factor that separated Jews and Christians is to be found rather in the Christian church. The synagogue did not expel the Christians; instead, the church rejected the Jews. At first, this rejection was only of a theological nature. It consisted of ideas expressing the superiority of the new

---

[8] Kimelman, "Birkat ha-Minim," 244.

[9] See Samson H. Levy, "The Best Kept Secret of Rabbinic Tradition," Judaism (1972): 462–69.

message of Christianity over the old Jewish faith. Then, very quickly the rejection shifted from the theological domain to the human one and focused on the Jewish people, who embodied rejection theology. Christian anti-Semitism was born.

Rejection of the Law

It is with the law that Christianity took its first steps outside Jewish soil. It is also because of the rejection of the law by Christians that Jews could no longer be open to the Christian message.

Whatever intrinsic value truth might have, the Jew could not accept it unless it met the ancient criterion: ". . . for teaching [torah] and for instruction? Surely, those who speak like this will have no dawn!" (Isaiah 8:20). Indeed, every day the Jew discovered in the law a definition of Jewish essence. To reject the law was nothing less than self-rejection and amounted to a pure betrayal: " 'If Israel does not accept the Torah,' says God to his angels, 'you and I can no longer subsist.' "[10] "The Holy One, blessed be he, covered the Israelites with Mount Sinai as with a cistern, and said to them: 'If you accept the Law, all is well; if not, there shall be your tomb' " (b. Shabbat 88a). These quotations from rabbinic literature, which are all the more interesting as they are more or less contemporary to the period of the separation, suggest Jewish self-defense.[11] "We can never abandon the law," was the Jewish response to Christian proselytism. "You might just as well ask us to deny our being and our God."

Historian Jules Isaac agrees: "The Jewish rejection of Christ was triggered by the Christian rejection of the Law. . . . The rejection of the Law was enough: to ask of the Jewish people that they accept this rejection . . . was like asking them to tear out their heart. His-

It is with the law that Christianity took its first steps outside Jewish soil.

---

[10] *Pesiqta Rabbati* 20; English translation of William G. Braude, *Pesikta Rabbati* (2 vols.; New Haven/London: Yale University Press, 1968), 1:406.

[11] On this question, see R. Travers Herford, *Christianity in Talmud and Midrash* (repr. Clifton, N.J.: Reference Book Publishers, 1966).

tory records no example of such a collective suicide."[12] Likewise, James D. G. Dunn notes: "Insofar as Judaism regarded the law . . . as integral to its identity, and continued to do so in a rabbinic Judaism which organized itself round the Torah, . . . a parting of the ways was inevitable."[13]

Even today, one of Judaism's most authoritative spokesmen, André Neher, states that messianic concepts, contrary to what one would expect, are not what separate Jew from Christian:

> A Jewish messianism carried to its ultimate consequences, this is how Christianity presents itself; and the theology of this messianism could be a subject of alarm only for a Jew accustomed to limited considerations. How many Jews with adventuresome souls, how many mystics among whom one could name more than one serious doctor of the Law, have touched the frontiers where the borderlines between Christianity and Judaism fade into unclarity as regards their resolve to remain true and faithful? We would say rather that they remained really true and faithful.[14]

Then, says Neher, if "irreconcilable divergences" exist between Christianity and Judaism, they must be sought at the level of the law.[15] On the Christian side, Harvey Cox also observes: "What divides Christians from Jews is not that we have different views of Jesus . . . What divides us is that Jews have something we do not. They have Torah."[16]

Rejection of the Sabbath

We must remember that the law at the center of the debate could not be the sacrificial laws of the Levitical cult. The temple being

[12] Jules Isaac, *Genèse de l'Antisémitisme: essai historique* (Paris: Calmann-Lévy, 1956), 147.

[13] James D. G. Dunn, *The Partings of the Ways: Between Christianity and Judaism and Their Significance for the Character of Christianity* (London: SCM/Philadelphia: Trinity, 1991), 139.

[14] André Neher, *L'Existence juive: solitude et affrontements* (Paris: Seuil, 1962), 236.

[15] Ibid. See also *Irreconcilable Differences? A Learning Resource for Jews and Christians*, ed. David F. Sandmel et al. (Boulder, Col.: Westview Press, 2001).

[16] Harvey Cox, "Rabbi Yeshua ben Yoseph: Reflections on Jesus' Jewishness and the Interfaith Dialogue," in *Jesus' Jewishness: Exploring the Place of Jesus within Early Judaism* (ed. James H. Charlesworth; New York: Crossroad, 1991), 45.

destroyed, sacrifices were no longer performed. And in Judaism as well as in Christianity sacrifices were regarded as no longer theologically relevant. The Jewish-Christian controversy over the law concerned, therefore, only a particular group of laws that remained relevant.

Among that particular group of laws, the Sabbath deserves the most attention because it became, more than any other law, the focus of the Judeo-Christian controversy. It was really in respect to the Sabbath that the two communities took up their opposing positions, to the point where, in Christianity, "sabbatize" was equivalent to "judaize."[17] The majority of Christians rejected the Jewish Sabbath and replaced it with the Christian Sunday, marking a complete distinction from Judaism.

> *The Sabbath deserves the most attention because it became, more than any other law, the focus of the Judeo-Christian controversy.*

The change started timidly at the end of the first century, as is evident from this isolated remark by Ignatius of Antioch: "Those who lived according to the old order have found the new hope. They no longer observe the Sabbath but the day of the Lord—the day our life was resurrected with Christ and by his death."[18]

However, at the time of the Marcionite heresy, in the second century, Christian reaction to identification with Jewish customs became important. Thus Marcion ordered fasting on Saturday: "Because it is the rest of the God of the Jews, who has created the world and has rested on the seventh day, we fast on that day in order not to accomplish on that day what was ordained by the God of the Jews" (Epiphanius, *Against Heresies* 42.3.4).

---

[17] Marcel Simon, *Verus Israel: A Study of the Relations between Christians and Jews in the Roman Empire (135–425)* (trans. H. McKeating; Oxford: Oxford University Press, 1986), 323 n. 69.

[18] Ignatius of Antioch, *Letter to the Magnesians* 9.1. The Greek text is susceptible to various translations, however, and one form of the text (that printed in Migne's *Patrologia Graeca*) indeed reads, "No longer sabbatizing, but living according to the *life* of the Lord."

The Christian reaction was reflected in the attitude of Bishop Victorinus de Pettau, in the third century, who did not want it to appear that he "observed the Sabbath of the Jews."[19]

The imperial councils of the fourth century were decisive. For the first time officially, due to the Christian obsession not to be identified with the Jews, the observance of Sunday was made official by decree.[20]

It seems clear, then, that because of its determination to disassociate itself from the Jews, Christianity rejected the observance of the biblical Sabbath.[21] Nor was it by chance that all this came to a head in the fourth century—the century of Constantine and the time when the church became the official religion of the state.

These two events are closely related historically. The church became a political power in the empire because of its marvelous ability to adapt. By rejecting the so-called Mosaic law and adopting Sunday as the day of worship (which was also a holy day for the Romans, who worshiped the sun),[22] Christianity greatly facilitated

---

[19] Victorinus, *On the Creation of the World*, in *The Ante-Nicene Fathers: Translations of the Writings of the Fathers Down to* A.D. 325 (ed. Alexander Roberts and James Donaldson; trans. Robert E. Wallis; repr. Peabody, Mass.: Hendrickson, 1995), 7:342.

[20] One finds the same concern at the Council of Nicaea (325 C.E.), when the issue came up in respect to Easter. Eusebius of Caesarea informs us of Emperor Constantine's opinion: "It appeared an unworthy thing that in the celebration of this most holy feast we should follow the practice of the Jews, who have impiously defiled their hands with enormous sin, and are, therefore, deservedly afflicted with blindness of soul. . . . Let us then have nothing in common with the detestable Jewish crowd"; Eusebius, *Life of Constantine the Great* 3.18–29, in *A Select Library of Nicene and Post-Nicene Fathers of the Christian Church* (ed. Philip Schaff and Henry Wace; 2d Series; Grand Rapids: Eerdmans, 1983), 1:524.

[21] Thus, among many other church historians, Augustus Neander noted: "The opposition to Judaism early led to the special observance of Sunday in place of the Sabbath"; *General History of the Christian Religion and Church* (trans. Joseph Torrey; 5 vols.; Edinburgh: T&T Clark, 1851), 1:402.

[22] Constantine's decree is clear: "The Emperor Constantine to Elpidius. Let all judges, the people of cities, and those employed in all trades, remain quiet on the Holy Day of Sunday. Persons residing in the country, however, can freely and lawfully proceed with the cultivation of the fields; as it frequently happens that the sowing of grain or the planting of vines cannot be deferred to a more suitable day, and by making concessions to Heaven the advantage of the time may be lost"; *Code of Justinian* 3.12.3 in

its task. Practically speaking, was it not better to discard the Sabbath in order to more freely evangelize the pagans? In the eyes of church leaders the church would become much stronger.

But to open one door was to close another. By rejecting the Sabbath, the church was indeed more successful among the pagans, who could now be incorporated en masse; but by eliminating the major obstacle in the way of the Gentiles, the church built a major one for the Jews.

For a Jew to abandon the Sabbath amounted to denying his or her own identity as a Jew. Josephus notes that "violating the Sabbath" was one of the greatest hallmarks of covenant disloyalty (*Jewish Antiquities* 11.346). Catholic and Protestant scholars have begun to realize this dilemma. Jean Cardinal Daniélou recognizes that "the change from Saturday to Sunday as the day of worship . . . made a choice between the two imperatives. It is understandable, in the light of the change, that conversion to Christianity could appear to Jews as a denial of Judaism.

For a Jew to abandon the Sabbath amounted to denying his or her own identity as a Jew.

This was a matter of conscience the importance of which I would not minimize."[23] From a Protestant perspective, Marvin Wilson describes this event forcefully:

> Over the centuries the Jewish community has interpreted the Church's decision to worship on Sunday as a rejection of the very heart of Jewish experience—rejection of the Law. This move to Sunday worship made it exceedingly difficult, if not virtually impossible, for the Jew to give any serious consideration to the Christian message. . . . The Jew saw the Church's move to Sunday worship as a call to abandon the Law and embrace a "new covenant" that had now replaced the "old covenant," which was thus declared ineffective and passé. In short, to become a

---

S. P. Scott, *The Civil Law, Including the Twelve Tables, the Institutes of Gaius, the Rules of Ulpian, the Opinions of Paulus, the Enactments of Justinian, and the Constitutions of Leo* (Cincinnati: Central Trust Company, 1932), 275.

[23] As quoted in Jacques Doukhan, *Drinking at the Sources: An Appeal to the Jew and the Christian to Note Their Common Beginnings* (trans. Walter R. Beach and Robert M. Johnston; Mountain View, Calif.: Pacific Press, 1981), 23.

Christian was considered as leaving behind the Jewishness of one's past, hardly a live option for any faithful Jew to consider.[24]

Rejection of Jews

The Genesis of Anti-Semitism. The story seems trivial. Yet, the move was significant. It is on the abandonment of the law, and more specifically the Sabbath, that the church triggered the parting of the ways. The historical record testifies that Christian preaching enjoyed enormous success among Jews up to the fourth century (see chapter 1 above), when the law and especially the Sabbath were formally rejected by the church. Is it a coincidence that this is also the time of the first seeds of Christian anti-Semitism? Historians have indeed established that the fourth century marks the beginning of hostile doctrines that nourished "the oldest hatred of human history." Among the most serious and violent texts against the Jews are those of Aphraates, Ephraem, Augustine, and Chrysostom. Laborious and remarkable research by church historian Marcel Simon brought him to the same conclusion: "The expansion of ecclesiastical anti-Semitism dates from the fourth century."[25]

> *It is on the abandonment of the law, and more specifically the Sabbath, that the church triggered the parting of the ways.*

Indeed, uniformity was not imposed overnight; at that time, the church was still struggling for its identity, but many scholars agree that "during the fourth century, the wheel had turned the full circle. From being persecuted, the Christians were now the persecutors."[26] Beginning with the fourth century, anti-Semitism developed into many forms.

---

[24] Wilson, *Our Father Abraham*, 80.

[25] Simon, *Verus Israel*, 263.

[26] W. H. C. Frend, *The Rise of Christianity* (Philadelphia: Fortress, 1984), 640. Cf. Timothy D. Barnes, *Constantine and Eusebius* (Cambridge, Mass.: Harvard University Press, 1981), 224.

In the beginning Christian anti-Semitism was essentially anti-Judaism; that is, it concerned itself with religion and expressed itself only in polemics and apologetics. Initially it contented itself with rhetorical figures and often delivered scathing maledictions on all who held to the law of Moses.[27] But at the end of the eleventh century, during the Crusades, anti-Semitism became for the first time "systematically" violent.[28] The massacres perpetrated by the Crusaders nearly always included the charge of deicide: "These Jews killed and crucified Jesus without any valid reason. Let us take vengeance on them and eliminate them from the bosom of the nations, so that none shall again remember the name of Israel."[29]

Not only did Jews receive a violent death at the hands of Christians; they also received a much more terrible, deeper, and enduring wound that has followed them to the present: their characterization as people with moneybags—practitioners of usury. This image of the Jew appeared for the first time during this period.

---

[27] As one example, among others, we may cite this letter of the Archbishop Agobard—a passage chosen from among the most violent of the epoch: "The men who are subject to the Mosaic Law are accursed and covered with the curse as by a garment, a curse which has soaked like water into their guts and like oil into their bones, cursed in the city and cursed in the field, cursed in their coming in and cursed in their going out. Cursed are the fruit of their body, of their ground, of their flocks, of their cellars, of their granaries, of their storehouses, of their sustenance and of the crumbs of their meals!" Letter to the archbishop of Narbonne, between 826 and 828 C.E.; cited by J. Régné, "Les juifs de Narbonne," *Revue des études juives* 55 (1908): 34. Cf. Léon Poliakov, *The History of Anti-Semitism* (trans. Richard Howard; 4 vols.; New York: Vanguard, 1965), 1:29–30.

[28] "In many ways 1096 marked a turning point in Jewish history. The trail of blood and smoldering ruins left behind in the Jewish communities from France to Palestine, . . . for the first time brought home to the Jewish people, its foes and friends, the utter instability of the Jewish position in the Western world. . . . Jews had encountered occasional outbreaks of intolerance. . . . But these 'incidents' invariably were local and sporadic in nature, lacked premeditation and widespread concerted action. From the First Crusade on, anti-Jewish persecutions exercised a dangerously contagious appeal, which in periods of great emotional stress degenerated into a mass psychosis transcending national boundaries"; Salo W. Baron, *A Social and Religious History of the Jews* (2d ed.; 18 vols.; New York: Columbia University Press, 1957), 4:89.

[29] Cf. Adolf Neubauer and Moritz Stern, *Hebräische Berichte über die Judenverfolgung während der Kreuzzüge* (repr. Hildesheim: Olms, 1997), 88.

Two factors played a role in producing this image. First, the cruel insecurity in which Jews found themselves encouraged them to change their possessions into a commodity such as silver or gold that could be easily concealed in case of danger. Inasmuch as money in those days was hard to come by, those who had it soon became lenders. Such was the position in which monasteries, too, found themselves.[30]

Second, Jews were forced by the circumstances of survival to do what Christians, in principle, were forbidden to do. Until then the Jews had listened to Jewish tradition and its spokesmen. On the eve of the first Crusade, the famous Jewish commentator Rashi was still of this opinion: "Whoever lends money to a foreigner on interest will be destroyed."[31] One century later the rabbis had to surrender to the inevitable. Wrote one rabbi: "In the present time, where Jews own no fields or vineyards whereby they could live, lending money to non-Jews for their livelihood is necessary and therefore permitted."[32] "In this sense," writes Fadiey Lovsky, "medieval society forced the Jew at least to practice usury, if not to engage in business."[33] For many generations, the only way to survive at all was by interest earned on money, a resource that consistently staved off violent death and expulsion.[34]

These circumstances created a Christian reaction of horror and repulsion. And Jewish reaction to such persecution further stirred up Christian hatred and contempt, creating a truly atrocious vicious circle.

But in the thirteenth century a yet more profound movement crystalized; the Jew was to become within the Christian society a

---

[30] Poliakov, *The History of Anti-Semitism,* 1:74.

[31] See James W. Parkes, *The Jew in the Medieval Community: A Study of His Political and Economic Situation* (2d ed.; New York: Sepher-Hermon, 1976), 341.

[32] Ibid.

[33] Fadiey Lovsky, *Antisémitisme et mystère d'Israël* (Paris: Michel, 1955), 233.

[34] "The loan of money . . . is the real motive for the tolerance of the lord who admitted the Jew, protected him, encouraged him, and then systematically exploited him and pitilessly fleeced him when the occasion presented itself, which was quite frequently" (L. Gauthier, "Les juifs dans les deux Bourgognes," *Revue des études juives* 49 [1904]: 14).

foreign element, and the ghetto was born.[35] In the fourteenth century came the myth that the Jew was "the devil in person."[36] The fifteenth and sixteenth centuries made the Jew a "pest"[37] that had to be destroyed. In the seventeenth century the word "deicide"[38] was reemphasized. From there, Christians did not have to go far to create the concept of Jews as a "foul race," which would find special attention in the pseudoscientific speculations of the nineteenth century.

In the eighteenth century, that century of light, it became possible for Jews, for the first time, to experience a mild form of emancipation, permitting them to mingle with citizens in general.

---

[35] It was the Lateran Council of 1215 which, by defining the status of the Jew as that of someone outside the law, determined the formation of the ghetto. The phenomenon did not exist previously; it became obligatory from that moment on.

[36] Jews were considered the incarnation of evil, and they were held responsible for all evils (plague, etc.) would be identified with the devil, especially in the fourteenth century.

[37] The expression is from Luther, who, after a notable friendliness toward Jews during his earlier career, turned violently against them in his later period; on this point, see Reinhold Lewin, *Luthers Stellung zu den Juden* (Berlin: Trowitzsch & Sohn, 1911). Cf. Luther's pamphlet *Against the Jews and Their Lies*: "In truth, the Jews, being foreigners, should possess nothing, and what they do posses should be ours. . . . To this day we still do not know what devil brought them into our country. . . . Aside from the Devil, you have no enemy more venomous, more desperate, more bitter, than a true Jew"; quoted in Poliakov, *History of Anti-Semitism*, 1:216–18. "On a practical level, Luther proposes a series of measures against the Jews: that their synagogues be burned, their books confiscated, that they be forbidden to pray to God in their own way, and that they be made to work with their hands; or, better still, that the princes expel them from their lands and that the authorities—magistrates as well as clergy—unite toward these ends. As for himself, having thus done his duty, Luther is 'excused' (*Ich habe das meine gethan: ich bin entschuldigt!*)"; Poliakov, *History of Anti-Semitism*, 1:218–19. In several passages, finally, Luther lamentably lets himself go into the most obscene buffoonery and gross vulgarities in lambasting the Jews, and he passes it all off as his most Christian sentiments.

[38] "That was, in the seventeenth century, the weightiest reproach in Christian opinion"; Lovsky, *Antisémitisme et mystère d'Israël*, 194. The sermons of Jacques Benigne Bossuet hammered it into the ears of Christians: "That which the Romans found intolerable for their citizens, the parricidal Jews have inflicted upon their King"; see also Poliakov, *History of Anti-Semitism*, 2:181.

Manners and customs, religion, and even the garb[39] that had until then distinguished the Jews tended to disappear. The traditional Jewish difference, however, was forced inward "to become a part of their very flesh, as though Western sensibility required the certainty of a distinction which, if ever superficially effaced, could subsist in an invisible essence."[40]

Thus the nineteenth century witnessed the appearance of racism—a new form of anti-Semitism resulting from a combination of circumstances favorable to its development.[41] The study of languages, then in full stride, influenced scientists to make a distinction between Aryans and Semites. The next step was for biologists to make this distinction (which originally was of language alone) into one of psychology and ethnology. The Semite and the Aryan (or Indo-German) were set against each other. The comparison was perceived as an advantage for the Aryan.

This desire to view Semites disadvantageously can be explained by the situation in Germany. The German people were still struggling to extricate themselves from the particularist and anarchist political system of the preceding centuries, which had made them into an assemblage of diverse peoples. They felt that the time had come to unify the German spirit and nation. Part of that effort was expended in an attempt to define more clearly what a German was. Germans had to be distinguished from a group they all recognized as foreign in their midst: the Jews. The situation became a confrontation between Semite and Aryan. In Germany, racist anti-Semitism became a national necessity.[42]

---

[39] As early as the Fourth Lateran Council it had been "decided that the Jews must distinguish themselves from the Christians by their dress"; cf. Fourth Lateran Council, Canons 67–70, in Joannes Dominicus Mansi, *Sacrorum conciliorum nova et amplissima collectio* (54 vols.; Graz: Akademische Druck, 1961), 22:1054–58.

[40] See Poliakov, *History of Anti-Semitism,* vol. 3.

[41] Cf. Arnold M. Rose, *L'origine des préjugés* (Paris: UNESCO, 1951), 15.

[42] As historian G. Barraclough rightly observes regarding the movement of National Socialism, "They offered a solution—specious but boldly enunciated—not only of the immediate evil of unemployment, but also of the two great unsolved problems which stood out as the enduring legacy of Germany's past: the problem of German unity and the problem of creating political institutions representative of the German people"; *The Origins of Modern Germany* (Oxford: Blackwell, 1957), 458.

The German people seem to need this thesis as a basis for national unity. Too bad, then, if historical truth stood in the way. "Even though it could be proved that there never was an Aryan race in the past," said Houston Chamberlain, who was one of the most fervent in accepting the Aryan doctrine, "there must be one in the future. For men of action this is a decisive point."[43]

Myth had supplanted truth; legend was right and history was wrong. Richard Wagner promoted this error in the very first of his writings, going so far as to resurrect the ancient god Woden and identify him with Christ: "Woden (Odin), the supreme god of the Germans, has not necessarily given his place to the God of the Christians; he can be positively identified with Him. . . . For in him is found, as in Christ, the Son of God, this decisive analogy: he also died, was wept for, and was avenged even as today we avenge Christ because of the actions of the Jews."[44] Aryan mythology fitted nicely into a Christian mold, including even the concept of deicide.

Wagner, though a pagan, could not exclude a religious justification of anti-Semitism. For him, the Jews represented civilization's "bad conscience" and "the hare to be hunted." It is not astonishing, therefore, that in concluding his resounding pamphlet "Judaism in Music," he suggests finally "the redemption of Ahasuerus—annihilation" as the only way to solve the Jewish problem.[45]

The Climax of Anti-Semitism. In the twentieth century, anti-Semitism reached its climax with the Holocaust. To be sure, the Holocaust emerged under the pressure of various economical, political, and historical factors. But no serious historian would today question the important connection between the sad history of the Christian "teaching of contempt" and the final solution promoted and accomplished by Hitler.

The Holocaust did not spring up by chance. It is the logical and unavoidable result of a long and consistent process within

---

[43] Houston S. Chamberlain, *Foundations of the Nineteenth Century* (New Orleans: Flanders Hall, 1988), 350–51.

[44] Quoted in Doukhan, *Drinking at the Sources*, 38.

[45] These sentiments echo the jibe of Luther: "If I find a Jew to baptize, I shall lead him to the Elbe bridge, hang a stone around his neck, and push him into the water, baptizing him with the name of Abraham!"; cited by Poliakov, *History of Anti-Semitism,* 1:223.

Christianity.[46] The traditional Christian belief that Judaism was superseded by the church, that the old Israel of the flesh was replaced by the new Israel of the spirit, made it possible for Christians to conclude that the Jews were superfluous and therefore to be eliminated. The so-called supersession or replacement theology contained the worst germs of hatred and potential murder and was rightly denounced as "a spiritual holocaust."[47] And the doctrine that the Jews had crucified the Son of God and were therefore rejected by God helped Christians to support and even to justify the death camps. Were Jews not cursed by God? All this served them right. But what is troubling is that this way of reasoning was and still is advocated by good Christians who did not support the Nazi regime and even fought against it. Even Dietrich Bonhoeffer, a hero of the resistance and a martyr to the Nazis, conceded that "the church of Christ has never lost sight of the thought that the 'chosen people,' who nailed the redeemer of the world to the cross, must bear the curse for its action through a long history of suffering."[48] This kind of statement had preceded and often accompanied the killing of the Jews. After the event, we now know how dangerous and unfair they are, yet these opinions are still preached from the pulpit and piously written in good Christian books.

> *The Holocaust did not spring up by chance. It is the logical and unavoidable result of a long and consistent process within Christianity.*

---

[46] On the connection between the Holocaust and Christian anti-Semitism, see Franklin Littell, *The Crucifixion of the Jews: The Failure of the Christians to Understand the Jewish Experience* (Macon, Ga.: Mercer University Press, 1986), 2, 30; Alice L. Eckardt and A. Roy Eckardt, *Long Night's Journey into Day: A Revised Retrospective on the Holocaust* (Detroit: Wayne University Press, 1982), 127.

[47] Darrell J. Fasching, ed., *The Jewish People in Christian Preaching* (New York: Mellen, 1984), x.

[48] Edwin H. Robertson, ed., *No Rusty Swords: Letters, Lectures and Notes, 1928–1936, from the Collected Works of Dietrich Bonhoeffer* (trans. Edwin H. Robertson and John Bowden; London: Collins/New York: Harper & Row, 1947), 1:226.

Still, many Christians refuse to recognize the connection between the horrible Holocaust and their Christian traditions and teachings. It is true that Nazism defined itself as an anti-Christian ideology with pagan overtones. Yet, this aspect of the Nazi propaganda was just a little nuance in the general anti-Semitic substance, for Christians were not put to death because they were Christians. They never wore a distinctive sign, a yellow cross, or something else to single them out for the purpose of deportation and genocide. Nazis were not anti-Jewish because they were anti-Christian. Instead they were anti-Christian insofar as they perceived Christianity in connection to the Jews. Their anti-Christianity was merely an expression of their fundamental anti-Semitism. It is also true that many Christians resisted the Nazi oppression and sometimes saved Jews at the price of their lives. Yet these acts of heroic righteousness were not systematic and were rather the exception than the rule. In general, Christianity kept silent before the crime, when it did not consciously or unconsciously support it. As someone once said, "Not all the Christians were the oppressors, but all the victims were Jews."

But even if many Christians did not share the Nazi ideology and fought against the Nazi power, it remains an undeniable fact that the anti-Semitic theses of the Nazi regime were directly borrowed from the traditional Christian teachings. Evidence is found in Nazi sources. Adolf Hitler himself confessed in his *Mein Kampf,* "I am acting in the sense of the Almighty Creator: By warding off the Jews I am fighting for the Lord's work."[49] In April 1933, he declared to two Catholic bishops who questioned his racial policy that "he was only putting into effect what Christianity had preached and practiced for 2000 years."[50]

It is significant indeed that notorious Nazi war criminal Julius Streicher quoted Luther in his defense at the Nuremberg Trials. A few years ago on Austrian television a former Nazi, now "repentant," explained how Jesus' crucifixion by the Jews had been taught to him repeatedly since his early youth and how this teaching

---

[49] Adolf Hitler, *Mein Kampf* (New York: Reynal & Hitchcock, 1941), 84.

[50] Cited by Rosemary R. Ruether, *Faith and Fratricide: The Theological Roots of Anti-Semitism* (New York: Seabury, 1974), 224.

helped distill in him a hatred that qualified him—even as an atheist—to become a member of the Hitler Youth.

These testimonies, along with many others, show that the Nazi destruction did not come out of the void, but was the natural culmination of a process. In order to prove this point Raul Hilberg sketches this process in these catching phrases: "1) In the fourth century Jews were told 'You have no right to live among us as Jews.' 2) From the Middle Ages to the nineteenth century, Jews were told 'You have no right to live among us.' 3) In the Nazi era, Jews were told 'You have no right to live.' "[51]

The church cut itself off from its Jewish roots. And the rejection of the Sabbath became the most concrete and formal expression of this move. As a result, anti-Semitism arose and evolved and ultimately climaxed in the Holocaust. This connection may seem exaggerated or somewhat unfair. Yet, history proves it right, and psychology confirms the diagnostic. It is the rejection of the roots that led to the murder of the parents. Says Marvin Wilson: "The most important reason the Holocaust happened is that the Church had forgotten its Jewish roots."[52]

It is the rejection of the roots that led to the murder of the parents.

Another important implication of the Christian rejection of Jews was that the Christian message was no longer made available to Jews. By rejecting its Jewish roots, the church lost the Jewish presence in its midst; the church lost the capacity and the right to witness to Jews.

---

[51] Raul Hilberg, *The Destruction of the European Jews* (Chicago: Quadrangle, 1961), 3–4.
[52] Wilson, *Our Father Abraham*, 101.

CHAPTER 3

THE CHRISTIAN REPLACEMENT

It was not just a rejection. Along with the theology of rejection, and because of it, a whole theology of replacement was developed by implication. In fact, the two ideas belong together. The technical name generally used to designate this system of thought, "supersessionism," accounts for these two ideas. The name comes from the Latin words *super* (on, upon) and *sedere* (to sit) and suggests that someone sits on the chair of another person, thus displacing the latter. Significantly, another name for this theory is "displacement theology," which implies that the old covenant with Israel has been abrogated and a new covenant has been set up in its place with the "new Israel." Displacement and abrogation belong together, so much so that Christian theologian Franklin Littell puts both aspects[1] under the same umbrella of supersessionism. The superseding myth has two foci: (1) God is finished with the Jews; and (2) the new Israel (the Christian church) takes the place of the Jewish people as the carrier of history.[2]

Supersessionist theology starts then along with rejection theology. Like the rejection theory, the supersessionist theory was not

---

[1] Systematic theologian R. Kendall Soulen calls the aspect of rejection "punitive supersessionism," which often accompanies "economic supersessionism," that is, the replacement of the "economy" of carnal Israel by the "economy" of the Church; *The God of Israel and Christian Theology* (Minneapolis: Fortress, 1996), 29–30.

[2] Franklin H. Littell, *The Crucifixion of the Jews* (New York: Harper & Row, 1975), 30.

propounded in apostolic teaching. In fact, Paul warns against it: "Do not boast over the branches. If you do boast, remember that it is not you that support the root, but the root that supports you" (Romans 11:18). Paul's severe admonition is explicit enough to suggest that the idea was already circulating among the early Christians. But it is especially the church fathers who "upon the deicide lie, based upon an Antisemitic distortion of the records of Jesus' trial and condemnation . . . went on to indulge in a 'high minded' boasting of precisely the kind that Paul warned them against."[3] According to Catholic theologian John Pawlikowski, this "theological reconstruction" is the root for "two long dominant trends in Christian thought":

> The first, which predominated in Catholicism (particularly in the liturgy), focused around the prophecy/fulfillment motif. Jesus fulfilled the Messianic prophecies of Judaism and thus inaugurated the messianic era for which Jews had hoped and prayed throughout the centuries. It was their own spiritual blindness that prevented most Jews from recognizing this fulfillment in the Christ Event. As a divine punishment for this blindness Jews were displaced in the covenantal relationship by those baptized into the "New Israel."[4]

The second trend, heavily identified with continental Protestant theology, saw freedom as the principal effect of the Christ event. Through his preaching and ministry and in a very special way through his death and resurrection, Jesus freed humankind from the "burden of Jewish Torah."

ECCLESIOLOGICAL SUPERSESSIONISM

The Church Replaces Israel

As John Pawlikowski points out, this trend of of the church replacing Israel was particularly prominent in Catholicism. The reason is simple. There the focus was ecclesiological and concerned

---

[3] Ibid., 29.

[4] John Pawlikowski, *Jesus and the Theology of Israel* (Wilmington, Del.: Michael Glazier, 1989), 10–11.

essentially the status of the church in relation to Israel. The best and perhaps the only way for the church to be credible in the eyes of the ancient world was to prove that it was the true heir of the heritage of Israel.

Justin Martyr and many other church fathers claimed that the church was the "true spiritual Israel," because "the Jews hardened their hearts and refused to understand the true meaning of the prophets."[5] The author of the *Epistle of Barnabas* urges Christians to assume their role as the new Israel.[6] Cyprian insists that since Jews have "forsaken the Lord and blasphemed the Holy One of Israel," Christians are now those who are allowed to call God " 'Our Father,' because He now has begun to be ours and has ceased to be of the Jews."[7]

Another rationale for supersessionism was the "missiological/political" concern of bringing Gentiles into the church. In the words of Isaac of Antioch in his *Homilies against the Jews*, the uncircumcised Gentiles have replaced Israel. And eventually as the church became the official religion of the Roman Empire, the concept of divine election was understood in political terms. In Eusebius's *Oration on Constantine,* Roman imperialism came ultimately to be identified with the reign of the Davidic Messiah.[8]

Churches Replace Synagogues

Replacement theology did not confine itself to the domain of rhetorics and theological apologetics; it also expressed itself through violent actions. Synagogues were attacked; and, what is more significant, they were replaced on the same premises by churches. The first recorded case was Bishop Innocentius of Dertona in northern

---

[5] Justin, *Dialogue with Trypho* 11, 12; see *Ante-Nicene Fathers* (ed. A. Roberts and J. Donaldson; 10 vols.; repr. Peabody, Mass.: Hendrickson, 1994), 1:199–200; cf. Ignatius, *To the Philadelphians* 5.2; translation in *The Apostolic Fathers* (ed. Michael W. Holmes; Grand Rapids: Baker, 1999), 179.

[6] *The Epistle to Barnabas,* translation in Holmes, ed., *The Apostolic Fathers,* 270–327.

[7] Cyprian, "The Lord's Prayer," in *Treatises* (ed. and trans. Roy J. Deferrari; New York: Fathers of the Church, 1958), 135.

[8] See Dan Cohn-Sherbok, *The Crucified Jew: Twenty Centuries of Christian Anti-Semitism* (Grand Rapids: Eerdmans, 1997), 31–32.

Italy, who died in 355 C.E.: "Under his rule, 'the Christians together with their bishop destroyed the synagogue, and erected a church on the site.' "[9] About the same period, "Christians also seized the Jewish synagogue of Tipasa in North Africa, and consecrated it as a church. Thirty years later they did the same at Rome."[10] In the East, the picture is not brighter. In Palestine a monk, Barsauma (around 400 C.E.), accompanied by forty monks destroyed several synagogues and consecrated them as churches.[11] Indeed, a great number of synagogues in both West and East were destroyed and transformed into churches. These Jews had not become Christians and, therefore, naturally and peacefully transformed their building to adjust it to their new Christian faith; rather, the process was violent and was perpetrated from outside, from a foreign origin. It is also highly significant that when this happened a special mass was celebrated to consecrate the buildings; and in this mass, Judaism was referred to in supersessionist terms, as "a deception that had been driven out."[12]

A few centuries later, the Crusades marked the second step in the painful history of Jewish-Christian relations. The avowed purpose of the Crusades was to take the Holy Sepulcher from the hands of the Muslims. Yet, it was Jews who suffered most from the Crusades. As early as 1094 C.E., Godfrey of Bouillon vowed that he would not participate in the Crusades until he had avenged the blood of Jesus by leaving no Jews alive. While economic factors as well as greed and booty were not absent, the primary motive was clearly the annihilation of the Jews as "God's worst enemies": "Let us, therefore, . . . extirpate them from among the nations, so that the name of Israel will no longer be mentioned."[13] On their way to the Holy Land and later when they reached Jerusalem (1099 C.E.), the Crusaders massacred Jews and in some places virtually exterminated them.

---

[9] James Parkes, *The Conflict of the Church and the Synagogue: A Study in the Origins of Antisemitism* (Cleveland: World, 1961), 187.

[10] Ibid.

[11] Ibid., 236.

[12] Robert Michael, "Antisemitism and the Church Fathers," in *Jewish-Christian Encounters over the Centuries: Symbiosis, Prejudice, Holocaust, Dialogue* (ed. Marvin Perry and Frederick M. Schweitzer; New York: Lang, 1994), 71 n. 13.

[13] Edward A. Synan, *The Popes and the Jews in the Middle Ages* (New York: Macmillan, 1965), 71.

The cross emblazoned on the tunic of each Crusader became the symbol of rallyment to liberate the Holy Land and Jerusalem from the infidels. Here again the theology of replacement was behind the holy war. Being the new, authentic Israel, Christians felt that they were the true legitimate heirs of the promised land. Marching toward the Holy Land, they identified themselves with the old Israel and believed that "God would divide the waters for this new exodus, and a purified Christianity would ensue."[14]

Supersessionism is both the most pernicious and the most lethal theory. It contributed more than any theory to the Holocaust.

In the fourth and fifth centuries, replacement theology led Christians to destroy synagogues and replace them with churches; now replacement theology led Crusaders to invade the Holy Land as their own property, hoping deep down in their hearts that "Jerusalem would become the religious capital for the Christian faith."[15] In each case, replacement theology was accompanied with violence and each time with the expressed intention to eliminate Jews from history. One day, this wish would find its ultimate perpetrator. The church fathers of the early centuries and the Crusaders of the Middle Ages paved the way for the ultimate crime. Littell's diagnostic is correct: "The genocidal note is already present in the superseding or displacement myths."[16] Supersessionism is both the most pernicious and the most lethal theory. It contributed more than any theory to the Holocaust. It is anti-Semitism at its best (or at its worst). Its psychological mechanism is clear: because you are what I want to be, I wish that you do not exist. And very soon, the crime or support of the crime would follow.

---

[14] Frederick M. Schweitzer, "Medieval Perceptions of Jews and Judaism," in *Jewish-Christian Encounters over the Centuries: Symbiosis, Prejudice, Holocaust, Dialogue* (ed. Marvin Perry and Frederick M. Schweitzer; New York: Lang, 1994), 133.

[15] Craig A. Evans and Donald A. Hagner, ed., *Anti-Semitism and Early Christianity: Issues of Polemic and Faith* (Minneapolis: Augsburg Fortress, 1993), 238.

[16] Littell, *Crucifixion of the Jews*, 30.

The Spirit Replaces the Flesh

The suspect nature of replacement theology is already betrayed in the language itself that expresses it. Indeed, the contrast between Israel of the flesh and spiritual Israel not only pertains to the dualistic thinking inherited from the gnostics and Marcion, but it also contributes to the traditional anti-Semitic portrayal of the Jew as a carnal figure. Augustine spoke of Jews as an "ungodly race of carnal Jews." Chrysostom went further along the same line and described Jews as "obstinate animals . . . fit for slaughter."[17] This dehumanization of the Jew "without soul" was one of the most prevailing themes in the church fathers' polemics. In the words of Robert Michael, "The Jew as he is encountered in the pages of fourth-century theologians and incorporated into Roman law is hardly human."[18]

Interestingly, the same ideas reappeared in pre-Nazi Germany and prepared for the ultimate "slaughter." German philosophers Kant and Schleiermacher emphasized "the sole legitimacy of the church by contrasting its spirituality with the carnal community of Jews.[19] Likewise, in 1886, French anti-Semite Edouard Drumont promoted the same racist propaganda, declaring that "the Semite is earthbound . . . the Aryan is a son of heaven."[20]

Replacement theology shaped the basis for the distorted views of Nazi ideology and thus prepared Christians to promote and allow the most horrible crime of human history.

THEOLOGICAL SUPERSESSIONISM

Grace Replaces Law

The most important theological implication of the replacement of Israel by the church concerns Christian reflection on the law. What makes Christianity radically different from and even opposed

---

[17] Michael, "Antisemitism and the Church Fathers," 114–15.
[18] Ibid., 116.
[19] Soulen, *God of Israel,* 79.
[20] Quoted in Cohn-Sherbok, *Crucified Jew,* 169.

to Judaism is that grace is now viewed in contrast to the law and has therefore replaced it. John Pawlikowski identified this theological trend especially in continental Protestantism: "The whole Jewish covenantal experience of the people's union with God through faithful observance of the Torah precepts integral to the divine-human bonding forged at Sinai was displaced by the *immediate,* individual covenantal union between the individual believer and God through Christ."[21]

And, indeed, from Reformer Martin Luther to New Testament Protestant theologian Rudolf Bultmann, one finds the same radical opposition between law and grace. For Luther, "the Law and the Gospel are two doctrines that are absolutely contrary."[22] For him, "the Law is the Word of perdition, the Word of wrath, the Word of sadness, the Word of pain, the voice of the Judge," while the Gospel "is the Word of salvation, the Word of grace, the Word of comfort, the Word of joy."[23] Likewise, in more modern and existential terms, Bultmann contrasts the "demand of the law" and the "demand of God" and comments that "the Christian faith *(pistis)* is not obedience to God's commandments, but obedience of faith to the way of salvation opened up in Christ."[24]

Even in recent Christian writings that are more sympathetic toward the Old Testament, the old Marcionite prejudice remains tenaciously alive. John Bright's discussion of the Old Testament laws is revealing: "The Law, as law, is ancient, irrelevant, and without authority. But what of the theology of the law? . . . The Law we cannot obey; but we are enjoined in all our dealings ever to strive to make the theology of the law actual."[25]

In order to appreciate the full impact of this Christian theology, it is also important to realize that this new emphasis has produced a new paradigm of thinking, a new mentality that now stands out

---

[21] Pawlikowski, *Jesus and the Theology of Israel,* 11.

[22] Ewald M. Plass, ed., *What Luther Says: An Anthology* (St Louis: Concordia, 1959), 2:733.

[23] Ibid., 732–33.

[24] Rudolf K. Bultmann, *Jesus and the Word* (trans. Louise P. Smith and Erminie H. Lantero; New York: Scribner, 1958), 31–33.

[25] John Bright, *The Authority of the Old Testament* (Nashville: Abingdon, 1967), 152–53.

versus the Jewish one. Emotions, sentimentality, and subjectivity now prevail over the reference of justice and the ethics and the value of practice. Significantly, Jewish philosopher Leo Baeck characterized Christianity as a "romantic religion" versus Judaism, which he calls a "classical religion."[26] In traditional Christianity, the God of the New Testament, Jesus, has been described as the God of love, the God who forgives, over against the God of the Old Testament, YHWH, who has been denounced as a jealous and demanding judge. As a result, the powerful God of history has been superseded by the kinder, gentler Jesus, by a cute, little Jesus of Christmas who does not threaten anyone.

Christianity has become a religion of ethereal feelings and abstract thinking versus the concrete and historical religion of the Hebrews.

The theology of salvation has also been affected by this shift. Whereas ancient Israelites were expecting a real objective action in history, Christians are rather interested in a spiritual, immediate, and subjective experience. On the human level, the hard requirements of ethics and the duty for righteous works have been replaced by an emphasis on Christian charity. Good sentiments are now more important than effective actions. Christianity has become a religion of ethereal feelings and abstract thinking versus the concrete and historical religion of the Hebrews. Historian of religion Joseph Kittagawa identifies Judaism with Asian religions in stark contrast to Christianity precisely on that observation: "If you ask Asians to describe their religion, they will tell you about their practices; if you ask Christians, they will tell you about their beliefs." "Judaism," concludes Kittagawa, "is in this respect more like an Asian religion than like Christianity."[27]

---

[26] See R. Travers Herford, "The Separation of Christianity from Judaism," in *Jewish Studies in Memory of Israel Abrahams* (New York: Arno, 1927), 204.

[27] From a private conversation reported in Jon D. Levenson, *The Hebrew Bible, the Old Testament, and Historical Criticism* (Louisville: Westminster John Knox, 1993), 52.

The New Testament Replaces the Old Testament

Given this claim that grace and the gospel have replaced the Torah, it is, therefore, not surprising that Christians tried to rid the church of the Hebrew Scriptures, or the "Old Testament," which witnessed to the Torah, and replaced it with the "New Testament," which witnessed to grace. This process started with Marcion in the middle of the second century, when he dissociated the two Testaments in his book *Antithesis*. So far, the sacred Scriptures consisted of only the Old Testament, to which Christians simply added more recent materials (see 2 Peter 3:15–16).[28] It is with Marcion that for the first time the New Testament writings were taken apart from the Old Testament Scriptures. New Testament scholar Norman Perrin remarks that "the very conception of a New Testament as distinct from the Old may well go back to Marcion's repudiation of the Jewish scriptures."[29] Patristic scholar Cyril Richardson confirms that, indeed, gnostic current played an important role in the shaping of the early church:

> *It is with Marcion that for the first time the New Testament writings were taken apart from the Old Testament Scriptures.*

> All Gnostic systems depend upon a principle that is at variance with Christianity—the dualism of matter and spirit. That the body was basically evil, and in no sense the creation of a good God, was a central tenet. It led Gnostics to dispute the underlying message of the Old Testament, and to contrast the creator-God with the God revealed in Jesus Christ. In consequence, as we have already seen, the Old Testament was rejected, and new Christian books were substituted in its place. It is interesting that not only the first New Testament canon comes from Gnostic sources, but Gnostics were the first to give New Testament passages the authority once enjoyed by the Old Testament (Basilides), to write a New Testament commentary (Heracleon), and to make a Gospel harmony

---

[28] See Robert Grant and David Tracy, *A Short History of the Interpretation of the Bible* (2d ed.; Philadelphia: Fortress, 1984), 40–41.

[29] Norman Perrin, *The New Testament: An Introduction* (New York: Harcourt Brace Jovanovich, 1974), 331.

(Tatian). This peculiar interest in a New Testament stems from the rejection of the Old.[30]

It is also highly instructive that gnostics appeared to have been the first "to provide relatively systematic exegesis of the New Testament."[31]

The church ultimately rejected Marcion's teaching to get rid of the Old Testament Scriptures, "but henceforth the Scriptures were divided into an Old and a New Testament, changing forever the way Christians would perceive their Scriptures."[32] From then on, the two Scriptures were regarded as two distinct entities, the "New" being considered superior over the "Old." It is interesting to note that the first usage of the technical expression "Old Testament" to refer to the Hebrew Scriptures[33] appears in fourth-century church father Eusebius of Ceasarea with the explicit intention to show the superiority of the New Testament over the Old Testament.[34] The first Old Testament theology was published by German theologian G. C. Bauer, who approached the Old Testament as a document distinct and separate from the New Testament. Bauer wrote his essay in 1796 with the definite presupposition that these two documents belonged to two different inspirations and that the Old Testament was in fact foreign to the Christian faith.

In modern times, in the years preceding the Nazi furor, church historian Adolf von Harnack called for the dismissal of the Old Testament and even denounced the Protestant practice of keeping the Old Testament in the Christian canon as "an ecclesiastical and

---

[30] Cyril C. Richardson, ed. and trans., *Early Christian Fathers* (Library of Christian Classics 1; Philadelphia: Westminster, 1953), 24–25.

[31] Grant and Tracy, *Short History of the Interpretation of the Bible*, 54.

[32] Clark M. Williamson, *A Guest in the House of Israel: Post Holocaust Church Theology* (Louisville: Westminster John Knox, 1993), 141.

[33] In 2 Corinthians 3:6, 14, the expressions "old testament" *(palaias diathēkēs)* and "new testament" *(kainēs diathēkēs)* refer to two covenants *(diathēkēs)*, as two frames of minds, two mentalities, two ways of reading the same revealed word, and do not yet imply two opposed written documents.

[34] See *The Ecclesiastical History of Eusebius Pamphilus, Bishop of Ceasarea, in Palestine* (trans. and intro. Christian F. Cruse; Philadelphia: Lippincott, 1887), 244–47.

religious paralysis."[35] Assyriologist Friedrich Delitzsch (not to be confused with his father Franz Delitzsch, a Hebrew scholar who translated the New Testament into Hebrew) wrote in *Die Grosse Täuschung* (1920) that the New Testament had superseded the Old Testament and that the Old Testament was definitely not a Christian book.[36]

More recently, New Testament theologian Rudolf Bultmann has again advocated clear Marcionite views.[37] Bultmann recognizes a historical link between the two Testaments. The New Testament "continues" the Old Testament; yet the Old Testament witnesses to a history of failure, a miscarriage *(scheitern)* of history. And it is this failure and especially the failure of obedience to the law that led to the necessity of grace. Again, we find here the classic opposition of law and grace familiar from Luther's theology and initiated by Marcion. Thus for Bultmann, it is clear that the Old Testament is nothing but a history of "miscarriage" and is therefore no longer a document relevant for the Christian faith.[38]

It is noteworthy that the neo-orthodox school of Karl Barth, who reacted to Bultmann's theology, still kept its distance from the Old Testament. Although Barth recognized the Christian's need for the Old Testament and the divine election of the Jewish people, he still opposed the God of grace of the New Testament to the God of law of the Old Testament. And the only theological value he was willing to recognize in the Old Testament is the extent that it would serve New Testament truth.[39]

---

[35] Adolf von Harnack, *Marcion: Das Evangelium vom fremden Gott eine Monographie zur Geschichte der Grundlegung der katholischen Kirche: Neue Studien zu Marcion* (Darmstadt: Wissenschaftliche Buchgesellschaft, 1960), 217.

[36] Friedrich Delitzsch, *Die grosse Täuschung* (Stuttgart: Deutsche Verlags-Anstalt, 1921), 95.

[37] See his article on *"Pisteuō,"* in *Theological Dictionary of the New Testament* (ed. Gerhard Kittel and Gerhard Friedrich; trans. Geoffrey W. Bromiley; 10 vols.; Grand Rapids: Eerdmans, 1964–1976), 6:174–228; see also Claus Westermann, *Essays on Old Testament Hermeneutics* (Richmond: John Knox, 1963), 849–57.

[38] Rudolf Bultmann, "Prophecy and Fulfillment," in *Essays on Old Testament Hermeneutics* (ed. Claus Westermann; English trans. ed. James L. Mays; Richmond: John Knox, 1963), 50–75.

[39] Karl Barth, *Church Dogmatics* (New York: Scribner, 1956), 112.

Another expression of supersessionist thinking is found in the traditional doctrine of "progressive revelation." This idea, which prevailed from the nineteenth century, is still defended, especially among conservative evangelical theologians. In fact, this theory was based upon a naturalistic view of the origins of biblical faith and proceeded, therefore, from an evolutionistic presupposition. According to this theory, the New Testament contained a more advanced and fuller form of revelation than the Old Testament, which was then qualified as a more primitive revelation and therefore no longer needed.[40]

Even the classical historical-critical method betrays the same vein of thinking, as far as it also implies the superiority of the more advanced over the more primitive. The Graf-Wellhausen idea that Hebrew history progresses from animism and primitive culture to a higher and more spiritual stage gave support to the general idea that Christian thinking was of a higher quality than that of the ancient Jews. Wellhausen's ideas belong to the anti-Semitic currents of his time; and as a result, at that time, "Orthodox Jewish scholars protested against the findings of these Christian higher critics, referring to their views as 'Higher Anti-Semitism.' "[41] Even today, Jon Levenson notes "that the critical study of the Hebrew Bible is itself often seen by Jews as inherently anti-Semitic."[42] Levenson warns: "We must not allow Wellhausen's theological liberalism and his anticlericalism to distract us from the degree to which he participated in the anti-Semitic culture of his time and place and failed to challenge its theological underpinnings. That his was not a racial anti-Semitism of the kind that flowered in Nazism should not blind us to the fact that his

> *Another expression of supersessionist thinking is found in the traditional doctrine of "progressive revelation."*

---

[40] See especially James Orr, *Revelation and Inspiration* (New York: Scribner, 1916).

[41] Cohn-Sherbok, *Crucified Jew*, 167–68.

[42] Levenson, *Hebrew Bible*, 43.

work 'made its modest contribution,' in Blenkinsopp's words, 'to the "final solution" of the Jewish problem under the Third Reich, a generation after his death.' "[43]

The pervasive presence in Christian circles of the supersessionist reading of the Bible is an interesting fact. As has been noted, this idea is found all across the spectrum of Christian orientations, from the most conservative and fundamentalist to the most liberal and critical approaches.

Sunday Replaces Sabbath

Christians did not just reject the Sabbath because they identified it as a ceremonial law and felt it was, therefore, no longer theologically relevant under the new covenant—they also replaced it with another day. But the very fact that they replaced it with another day shows already an internal contradiction in Christian theological reasoning. If the law of the Sabbath belongs to the ceremonial system and is no longer binding, why replace it with another day? This paradox shows how much the theology of replacement played a determining role in that process. The new day is in fact given as an expression of this replacement. Augustine (354–430 C.E.) provides the reason for the origin of Sunday in those terms: "The Lord's day was not declared to the Jews but to the Christians by the resurrection of the Lord and from that event its festivity had its origin."[44] In another letter, the same author states: "The Lord's day has been preferred to the Sabbath by the faith of the resurrection."[45]

The two theological reasons for the observation of each day are explicitly enunciated in order to justify both celebrations. First, Sunday came along with Sabbath: "The Sabbath is on account of the creation, and the Lord's day of the resurrection."[46] Yet, very

---

[43] Ibid., 42.

[44] Augustine, *Epistula* 55.23.1 (Corpus scriptorum ecclesiasticorum latinorum 34:194), as quoted by Samuele Bacchiocchi, *From Sabbath to Sunday: A Historical Investigation of the Rise of Sunday Observance in Early Christianity* (Rome: Pontifical Gregorian University Press, 1977), 270.

[45] Augustine, *Epistula* 36.12.14 (Corpus scriptorum ecclesiasticorum latinorum 34:4), as quoted by Bacchiocchi, *From Sabbath to Sunday*, 270–71.

[46] *Apostolic Constitutions* 8.33.1, translation from *Ante-Nicene Fathers*, 7:495.

quickly, following the supersessionist principle, the new day is given as a better anniversary and a day superior over the old Sabbath, for "the Sabbath was the end of the first creation, the Lord's day was the beginning of the second in which he renewed and restored the old."[47] Sabbath and Sunday are here contrasted as symbols of the old and the new economies. The new represents, of course, a higher and more complete form of religion.

Likewise, in the *Epistle of Barnabas* (ca. 130 C.E.), Sunday marks "the beginning of another world."[48] For that matter, Sunday is then called the "eighth day." It is noteworthy that this denomination, which is used here for the first time,[49] will be used over and over by early Christian authors who want to emphasize the contrast between the spiritual Sunday and the materialistic Sabbath.

Among them, the gnostics deserve a special mention since, as Jean Cardinal Daniélou pointed out, they "were carried away by this theme [i.e., eighth day]."[50] Sunday became then the symbol of a higher spirituality as illustrated in a text reported by Clement of Alexandria (ca. 150–215 C.E.): "The rest of the spiritual men takes place on the day of the Lord . . . in the ogdoad which is called the day of the Lord."[51]

Origen continues the same tradition in his commentary on Psalm 118 when "he presents the seventh day as a sign of matter, of impurity and of uncircumcision, while to the eight day he reserves the symbol of perfection, of spirituality and of purification by the new circumcision provided by Christ's resurrection."[52] Likewise for Bishop Ambrose of Milan (ca. 339–397 C.E.), the Jewish Sabbath is the sign of this world, whereas the eighth day is the sign of the grace

---

[47] Athanasius, *De sabbatis et circumcisione* 4 (Patrologia graeca 28.133), as quoted in Bacchiocchi, *From Sabbath to Sunday,* 276.

[48] See Edgar J. Goodspeed, *The Apostolic Fathers: An American Translation* (New York: Harper & Brothers, 1950), 41.

[49] Probably under the influence of the book of Enoch. See Bacchiocchi, *From Sabbath to Sunday,* 282.

[50] Jean Daniélou, *The Bible and Liturgy* (Notre Dame: University of Notre Dame Press, 1956), 258.

[51] Clement of Alexandria, *Excerpta ex Theodoto* 63.1 (Sources chrétiennes 23:185), as quoted by Bacchiocchi, *From Sabbath to Sunday,* 287.

[52] See Origen, *Selecta in Psalmos* 118, 164 (Patrologia graeca 12:1588), as quoted in Bacchiocchi, *From Sabbath to Sunday,* 289.

"which made man not of this world but of above."[53] Bishop Basil of Caesarea (ca. 330–379 C.E.) regards the eighth day as a figure of the "future life," "outside the time of the seven days."[54]

The change of Sabbath to Sunday in early Christianity was not just a historical accident due to the influx of Gentile converts who came from a Sunday-worship environment. It was also an expression of the Christian theology of replacement.

Salvation Replaces Creation

Christian overemphasis on salvation against creation originated, in fact, in Marcion, who opposed salvation to creation, the Savior to the Creator, the two Beings being exclusive.[55] Since that time, this thought has prevailed in Christian theology. In the nineteenth century, philosopher Ludwig Feuerbach described Christian thinking in these terms: "Nature, the world, has no value, no interest for Christians. The Christian thinks only of himself and the salvation of his soul."[56]

The change of Sabbath to Sunday in early Christianity . . . was also an expression of the Christian theology of replacement.

Generally, Old Testament scholars like to place the focal point of Israel's religion in the Exodus deliverance from Egypt,[57] from

---

[53] Ambrose, *Explanatio Psalmi* 47 (Corpus scriptorum ecclesiasticorum latinorum 64:347), as quoted by Bacchiocchi, *From Sabbath to Sunday*, 291.

[54] Basil, *In Hexaemeron* 2.8 (Sources chrétiennes 180), as quoted by Bacchiocchi, *From Sabbath to Sunday*, 296.

[55] See Westermann's discussion on creation and redemption in *Essays on Old Testament Hermeneutics*, 113–23.

[56] Ludwig A. Feuerbach, *The Essence of Christianity* (trans. George Eliot; New York: Harper, 1957), 287.

[57] See for instance Gerhard von Rad, "Das theologiche Problem des alttestamentlichen Schöpfungsglaubens," in *Gesammelte Stududien zum Alten Testament* (München: C. Kaiser, 1965), 136; Theodorus C. Vriezen, *An Outline of Old Testament Theology* (Oxford: Blackwell, 1966), 187–89; and Claus Westermann, *The Praise of God in Psalms* (Richmond: John Knox Press, 1965), 126 n. 78.

which was derived the secondary idea of creation. This presupposition is, in fact, behind the idea generally defended by critical scholars, namely that the creation story (Genesis 1:1–2:4a, the P-source) is nothing but a postexilic work[58] produced out of the exilic theology of redemption. Likewise, systematic theologians like Barth, Brunner, and others, have each one in his own way developed his philosophy of creation within the same paradigm from redemption to creation.[59]

These samples of theological thinking, among many others, attest clearly to the significant trend in Christian reflection on creation. Indeed, since Marcion, Christians have not only opposed creation to salvation, but they have also valorized salvation over creation.

This conceptualization has gone far beyond the borders of professional theoreticians of Christian theology. It has produced a dualistic mentality that has had a profound impact on our civilization. Henceforth, the physical world was opposed to the spiritual one. The Hebrew positive view of creation with its affirmation of life and of the human body was replaced by the Christian valorization of death, suffering, and despisement of anything appealing to the sensual enjoyment of physical life.

THE JEWISH-CHRISTIAN POLARIZATION

The Jewish-Christian tragedy is not just about the wounds of Israel and the forgetfulness of the church. Christian and Jewish identities have been affected in the process.

By rejecting its Jewish roots and replacing them by new ones of its own, Gentile Christianity has not only initiated and forced the parting of the ways, it has also produced a Christian identity deliberately set up against the Jewish one. And as a result, the Jews displayed a similar reflex. Indeed, the two religions shaped much of their respective identities in reaction to each other.

---

[58] Jacques Doukhan, *The Genesis Creation Story: Its Literary Structure* (Berrien Springs, Mich.: Andrews University Press, 1978), 140–53.
[59] Ibid., 190–93.

It is no exaggeration to say that Jews and Christians alike have forged a good part of their respective theology, culture, and mentality in conscious opposition to each other. One might even wonder if they now do not owe some of their very identity to this age-long clash.

Jewish scholar Michael Wyschogrod has recognized this phenomenon and, considering the process through which Jews and Christians have shaped their theological identity, concludes: "The effect has been a kind of polarization. . . . we have here a situation in which both faiths have damaged one another."[60]

To recover their original and authentic identity, Jews and Christians should, therefore, take the lessons of history and liberate themselves from this reflex of reaction formed through the ages. Their destiny, their identity, and even their mission depends on that.

As long as the Christian proclamation of the good news for all nations is accompanied with "bad news" for Jews; as long as the Christian truth of the salvation of the world resounds with the traditional Christian "teaching of contempt" and the rejection of Jews; as long as Christians refuse to recognize their Jewish roots and do not "remember that it is not you that support the root, but the root that supports you" (Romans 11:18); as long as Christians ignore the testimony of the Jews and their sacred deposit, according to the Apostle Paul "the adoption, the glory, the covenants, the giving of the law, the worship, and the promises," but also "the patriarchs, and from them, according to the flesh, comes the Messiah" (Romans 9:4–5)— as long as they do all this, Christians are in fact denying their own

> *It is no exaggeration to say that Jews and Christians alike have forged a good part of their respective theology, culture, and mentality in conscious opposition to each other.*

---

[60] Michael Wyschogrod, "A Jewish View of Christianity," in *Toward a Theological Encounter: Jewish Understandings of Christianity* (ed. Leon Klenicki; New York: Paulist, 1991), 113–14.

existence as Christians, for Christianity is in essence Jewish or it is not Christianity.

On the other hand, as long as Jews refuse to read the New Testament; as long as Jews fear to hear or speak or learn about Jesus with the idea that this may threaten their faithfulness to Jewish identity; as long as Jews insist in defining Jews in opposition to Christians and does not have the courage or simply the tolerance to include among Jews those who read the New Testament and to accept them at their side in the synagogue and in Israel—as long as they do all this, Jews still betray their insecurity as Jews. This automatic emotional rejection based on centuries of suffering and oppression paradoxically suggests that Jewish thinking and spiritual destiny are still dependent on Christianity.

What is at stake here goes beyond the two religions themselves, as cultural and historical phenomena. It concerns, in fact, the very reason for their existence, their supernatural claim, and hence their mission. If their truth is the mere result of a human process of reaction, then the authority of this truth is in question. For in this process, they have not only hurt the means that make their mission possible—they are no longer able to receive from each other—but more importantly they have also lost their credibility as witnesses to the absolute and universal revelation from above, which makes their mission necessary.

CHAPTER 4

MISSION IMPOSSIBLE

And now, the so-called mission to the Jews has become one of the most dramatic ironies of the Christian mission. Originally, Jews were the first target of the Christian proclamation. One of the strongest statements about this priority of the Jews was pronounced by Jesus himself. To a Greek woman who begged for his salvation, he unambiguously responded: "Let the children be fed first, for it is not fair to take the children's food and throw it to the dogs" (Mark 7:27). And, indeed, the woman got the message; she identified herself with "the dogs under the table" who are allowed to "eat the children's crumbs" (Mark 7:28). And later, Jesus commissions his disciples: "Go nowhere among the Gentiles, and enter no town of the Samaritans, but go rather to the lost sheep of the house of Israel" (Matthew 10:5–6). The Apostle Paul echoes this principle when he affirms that salvation is "to the Jew first" (Romans 1:16). And, indeed, the Jews were not only the first "Christian" missionaries to the world, but because of that they were also the first population to be reached by the Christian message. Catholic theologian Eugene Fisher acknowledges that even after "the first Christian Pentecost, the followers of Jesus continued to consider themselves as Jews and to address their message to their fellow Jews (Acts 2:14, 22, 29, 36, 42–47)."[1] And yet, the history of the Christian mission took a different direction altogether. In the beginning, the mission to the Jews was successful and many thousands and myriads of Jews

---

[1] Eugene J. Fisher, "Historical Developments in the Theology of Christian Mission," in *Christian Mission-Jewish Mission* (ed. Martin A. Cohen and Elga Croner; New York: Paulist, 1982), 7.

welcomed the Christian message. But suddenly, after the fourth century, the mission stopped dramatically. Preaching and arguing became insufficient, so much so that the Christian mission resorted to force and governmental persecutions; taxation and discriminatory laws became commonplace in the medieval world. Finally, the mission to the Jews became the last and most difficult of the Christian missions.

This failure after such brilliant and promising beginnings is puzzling and calls for reflection. It means that something changed radically in the Christians' testimony to the Jews, something that made the Christians unable to function adequately and efficiently in their mission to the Jews.

THE MISSION OF THE CHRISTIANS

The main reason for the failure of the Christian mission is to be found within the subject of the mission—the Christians themselves. Even Luther with all his venom against Jews recognized that "if I had been a Jew and had seen such boors and brutes control and teach the Christian faith, I would rather have become a sow than a Christian."[2] Likewise, Herbert Danby, writing on "the Jewish attitude towards Christianity," realized what he called "our failure as a Church." In his words, "the Church, by its deliberate choice and conduct, has made itself one gigantic and seemingly impenetrable obstacle between them and the figure of our blessed Lord."[3] Jewish-Christian theologian Jacob Jocz calls the church "the first and foremost stumbling-block in the Jewish appreciation of Jesus."[4]

The failure is caused by the fact that the church has come out of Israel and, therefore, Christians have lost touch with Jews. The

---

[2] See Martin Luther, *What Luther Says: An Anthology* (ed. Ewald M. Plass; St. Louis: Concordia, 1959), 2:683.

[3] Herbert Danby, *The Jew and Christianity: Some Phases, Ancient and Modern, of the Jewish Attitude towards Christianity* (London: Sheldon, 1927), iii, 38.

[4] Jakob Jocz, *The Jewish People and Jesus Christ: A Study in the Controversy between Church and Synagogue* (London: SPCK, 1962), 92.

church is almost exclusively made of Gentiles; and since the separation, the message concerning Jesus as a Jewish Messiah has been carried by non-Jews. How can a Jew hear about a Jewish truth from someone who is not a Jew? This language of common sense may sound arrogant to some Christians who think that truth should be enough to convince—regardless where it comes from. Yet, they ignore the important principle of the relationship between message and messenger. Indeed, Christian truth is perceived by Jews as a foreign truth because it is conveyed through foreign channels. As such, Christian truth is suspected as an attempt to alienate the Jew. And, indeed, the result betrays the intention. In order to become a Christian, Jews are told that they have to abandon their Jewish identity. They have to adopt another culture, another religious language, other forms of worship and prayer, another literature, another lifestyle, another food, even another history, and forget about their own glorious history and the reference to their fathers and their traditional wisdom.

> *In early Christianity, the question was debated whether a Gentile had to become a Jew in order to become a Christian. . . . The paradox is that now this question is not even debated: the Jew must become a Gentile in order to become a Christian.*

In early Christianity, the question was debated whether a Gentile had to become a Jew in order to become a Christian. And the heart of the discussion recorded in Acts 15 shows how serious the dilemma was. The paradox is that now this question is not even debated: the Jew must become a Gentile in order to become a Christian.

Also, the quality of the motivation of Christians who want to convert Jews is tested here. Are Christians really concerned with the welfare of Jews, with the salvation of Jews, or are they rather moved by the subtle temptation to transform Jews into their own Christian image? Unfortunately, the facts seem to point to the latter, since the conversion of Jews implies, even requires, the abandonment of their Jewish identity. This motivation directly implicates the Christian theology of replacement or supersessionism. Since I am the true Israel—that is, what you think you are—you should therefore no longer be what you are, but become what I am. This is the message of the theology of replacement; and this is, indeed, what Christian missionaries have traditionally attempted to achieve—to make Jews into "Gentiles" like them. Because Christian truth has been carried by non-Jews, and because it obliged Jews to become non-Jews—and the two propositions are related—the Jews cannot, they should not, accept it as a truth, let alone as a Jewish truth. The Christian mission to Jews is therefore illegitimate and bound to fail. In fact, it failed for that very reason.

But there is more. Christians who carried this truth to the Jews were not just foreigners, not just Gentiles. For the Jews, Christianity became the sworn enemy of Israel. This enemy has even been identified in Jewish tradition "as the incarnation of Rome, symbolized by Edom or Esau, and as the evil power of the world bent on destroying Jacob."[5] Christian cruelty, frenzied massacres, and the systematic teaching and preaching of contempt still resound in Jewish ears. The wounds are far from being healed, much less forgotten. The wounds are still perpetrated and renewed by the tenacious, subtle, invasive anti-Semitism, which ever carries within it the ferments of unforgivable genocide. Christianity has caused too many victims in Israel for the Jews suddenly to forget and consent serenely to dialogue—still less to convert.

Even the religious and theological motivation that may justify the Christian mission, the claim for the truth itself is questionable. Beginning with the first centuries, and particularly with the fourth, Christianity appeared more and more to the Jew not just as a foreign philosophy or as an evil and wicked power, but more seriously as a false religion. The reason for the Jewish refusal of the Christian message was not just cultural, because it looked strange or human or because the Jews were oppressed. Jews could not accept the

---

[5] R. J. Zwi Werblowsky, "Christianity," *Encyclopaedia Judaica* (16 vols.; New York: Macmillan, 1971), 5:514.

Christian truth for theological reasons—it did not correspond to the revealed criteria of the "Law and the Prophets." The truth about the Messiah was not enough. However great, beautiful, and right this truth may be, if it happens to contradict the Torah, the revelation from above given to Israel through Moses, then this truth is deemed to be a truth that does not come from the God of Israel. If Christian grace has put an end to Jewish law; if the Christian Sunday has abrogated the Jewish Sabbath; if the reference to a visible God ever suspended on a cross has replaced the reference to the invisible Almighty; if salvation and its emphasis on the spiritual has prevailed over creation, nature, and the body; if the New Testament has done away with the Old Testament; if the Gentiles have superseded Israel—then the Jews were and still are theologically right to turn down the Christian religion.

History has confirmed that this move in Christianity, the Christian rejection of the law and of its Jewish roots, led to the Jewish rejection of Jesus as the Messiah. It is, indeed, significant that as long as Christianity remained rooted in the Jewish soil, as long as the Torah was still a part of Christian life, Jews had no problem considering the messiahship of Jesus. We have already noted in that respect the crucial turning point of the fourth century that marked the definitive separation between the church and Israel. Christian historian James Parkes speaks of "the significant contribution of the fourth century to Jewish Christian relationships."[6] Significantly, Jewish scholar Jacob Neusner contends that in the fourth century the two religions shaped their respective identities:

> In the fourth century C.E., beginning with the conversion of Constantine in 312 and ending with the recognition of Christianity as the religion of the Roman Empire in the Theodosian Code of 387, Christianity reached that position of political and cultural dominance that it would enjoy until the twentieth century. In the fourth century, in response to the triumph of Christianity in the Roman Empire, Judaism as shaped by sages in the Land of Israel defined its doctrines.[7]

---

[6] James Parkes, *The Conflict of the Church and the Synagogue: A Study in the Origins of Antisemitism* (Cleveland: World, 1961), 174.

[7] Jacob Neusner, *Jews and Christians: The Myth of a Common Tradition* (London: SCM/Philadelphia: Trinity, 1991), 30.

No wonder that the fourth century marked the birth of the conflict between the church and Israel. Historian Jules Isaac finds in the fourth century the portents of the great persecution of the Jews:

> A great and surprising revolution, deplored by some, praised by others, one of the most important in history, of which the reign of Constantine was only the prelude, which continued and was consummated by end of the century, the extraordinary and chaotic fourth century. But the unheard of fortune of the Church brought in its train the misfortune of the Synagogue; for the fourth century was a fatal epoch, which opened up a future of anguish, mourning, and catastrophes."[8]

The reasoning is then simple and rigorous: since failure of the Christian mission to the Jews starts essentially from the fourth century, and since the fourth century marks also the starting point of Christian anti-Semitism and of the official rejection of the law, it follows that the first cause for the failure of the Christian mission to the Jews is to be found in Christianity.

THE MISSION OF THE JEWS

The second reason for the failure of the Christian mission is the mission of the Jews itself. In order to follow the Jesus presented by the Christians, the Jews had to abandon all the spiritual and culture heritage they had received from their ancestors. The conversion of Jews would then ultimately lead to elimination of Jewish life with all its treasure and the testimony that played a vital role even for the survival of Christian life and identity. Abraham Heschel describes this tragic eventuality in moving words:

> Is it really the will of God that there be no more Judaism in the world? Would it really be the triumph of God if the scrolls of the Torah would no more be taken out of the Ark and the Torah no more read in the Synagogue, our ancient Hebrew prayers in which Jesus himself worshiped no more recited, the Passover Seder no more celebrated in our lives, the law of Moses no more observed in our homes? Would it really be *ad Majorem Dei gloriam* to have a world without Jews?[9]

---

[8] Jules Isaac, *Genèse de l'Antisémitisme: Essai historique* (Paris: Calmann-Lévy, 1956), 156.

[9] Abraham Heschel, "No Religion Is an Island," *Union Seminary Quarterly Review* 21 (November 1965): 129.

In other words, the very reason for their refusal is the reason for their survival. The Jews rejected the Christian message because it implied the rejection of their own spiritual heritage. Their faithfulness to Torah saved them and made their testimony necessary for the salvation of the Christians. It is interesting that this way of reasoning served as the major argument in the papal legislation to protect the Jews. As Edward Synan has shown in his work *The Popes and the Jews in the Middle Ages:* "There is no moment, . . . when Christian legislation on the Jews is silent on their providential role, especially as guardians of Scripture."[10] One example of this spiritual dependence of Christianity on the Jews is found in an address by Pope Innocent III (1198–1216) to the count of Nevers where he argues that

> *The very reason for their refusal is the reason for their survival.*

the Jews "ought not to be slain lest the Christian people forget divine Law."[11] Catholic theologian Eugene Fisher echoes this concern in what he calls "a startling admission": "The notion of Jews functioning to remind Christians of the Law presumes their existence, not as potential converts, but precisely as Jews."[12] And he goes so far as to recognize with Abraham Heschel that "the Church's essential mission in and to the world would be crippled without a living Jewish witness to the truth of God's Torah."[13]

The Jewish witness to God's Torah is all the more necessary since Christians have largely abandoned this law. The reason for the church's failure is, then, the reason for Israel's success: Israel survived in order to preserve what has been rejected by the church. It would seem, then, that the conversion of Jews, which is the objective of many Christian missions, has for prerequisite the conversion of the Christians. The so-called mission to the Jews is first of all a mission to the Christians.

---

[10] Edward A. Synan, *The Popes and the Jews in the Middle Ages* (New York: Macmillan/London: Collier-Macmillan, 1965), 19.

[11] Ibid., 226.

[12] Fisher, "Historical Developments in the Theology of Christian Mission," 26.

[13] Ibid.

Only when Christians engage in genuine *teshuvah*, return to their Jewish roots, their original roots, and reappreciate the value of Torah, not only as a theological or spiritual exercise, but as a concrete fact of their existence; only when Christians recognize the evil nature of anti-Semitism and do everything to eradicate it from their hearts, their mouths, and their doctrines; only when Christians recognize the theological right of Jews to be Israel and not claim at the same time that Christians are the "true," the "spiritual," and the "new" Israel that has replaced the old one; only when Christians recognize and respect the cultural and also the religious identity of the Jews, even those Jews who have joined them in their faith and their messianic hope, and do not try to alienate them, to transform them into their image and oblige them to worship, think, and behave the way Christians are used to, but instead learn from them in order to enrich their own Christian experience and refresh their Jewish roots; only when the church is bold and humble enough to be grafted again into the antique olive tree—only then will Jews consider Christianity afresh—and respect it.

Catholic theologian John Pawlikowski dares to envisage this possibility. For him, the conversion movement among Christians may well bring along a similar movement among Jews: "Sooner or later these changes, if accepted by Christianity at large, will force Jews to reconsider some of their traditional outlooks on the Jewish-Christian bond from their side."[14] In her book on Christian anti-Semitism, *Faith and Fratricide,* Rosemary Ruether infers the same lesson; for her the key event is the return of Christians to the older sibling Judaism.[15] This whole scenario of the church and Israel drawing near to each other, instead of their traditional reacting to and moving away from each other, appears to be merely a utopia; and considering the weight of history today after the Holocaust and the creation of the state of Israel, this double mission seems impossible. To speak about the Judaization of the church after these two-thousand years of rejection sounds ludicrous and unbelievable. To

---

[14] John Pawlikowski, *Jesus and the Theology of Israel* (Wilmington, Del.: Glazier, 1989), 98.

[15] Rosemary R. Ruether, *Faith and Fratricide: The Theological Roots of Anti-Semitism* (New York: Seabury, 1974), 254–57.

speak about the conversion of Jews after the Holocaust and the creation of the state of Israel when Jewish identity has become more than ever such a precious value sounds indecent and unbearable.

AFTER AUSCHWITZ AND JERUSALEM

Yet, history has such ironies. Paradoxically the Holocaust and the creation of the state of Israel have produced a new climate for the Jewish-Christian encounter.

The Holocaust has revealed to the church the nature of its iniquity and through this new shame obliged Christians to rethink their relationship with Jews. As Alice Eckardt notes, "It took the German Nazis' 'final solution' to make the Christians begin to be aware that the so-called Jewish problem is in reality a Christian problem and that it has always been so."[16] Indeed, the horror of the Holocaust has shaken and awakened Christian sensitivity and made more and more Christians aware of the dangers and even the errors of much of their traditional teachings. The Holocaust has been qualified as "the most profound shaping event for Christian theology."[17]

Johannes Metz has encapsulated this impact of the Holocaust on Christian theology in his appeal to Christian theologians: "What Christian theologians can *do* for the murdered of Auschwitz and thereby for a true Christian-Jewish ecumenism is, in every case, this: Never again to do theology in such a way that its construction remains unaffected, or could remain unaffected, by Auschwitz."[18]

James Moore moves the reflection to the issue of hermeneutics: "Any interpretation of Christian scripture holds up in the face of the questions shaped by the events of the Shoah. Interpretations that

---

[16] Alice L. Eckardt, "A Christian Problem: Review of Protestant Documents," in *More Stepping Stones to Jewish-Christian Relations: An Unabridged Collection of Christian Documents, 1975–1983* (ed. Helga Croner; New York: Paulist, 1985), 16.

[17] James F. Moore, *Christian Theology after the Shoah* (Studies in the Shoah 7; Lanham, Md.: University Press of America, 1993), 25.

[18] Johannes Baptist Metz, *The Emergent Church: The Future of Christianity in a Postbourgeois World* (trans. Peter Mann; New York: Crossroad, 1981), 28.

are unable to hold in the light of that challenge must be considered suspect."[19] This theological awareness has thus drawn Christians closer to Jews, but also to Judaism. Christians are becoming more interested in Jewish studies and in the theological content of the Hebrew Scriptures.

One of the most significant implications of this interest concerns the Christian view of the mission to the Jews. Referring to the Holocaust, Protestant and Catholic theologians are increasingly questioning the propriety of efforts to convert Jews.

The survival of Jews as Jews is then necessary not only for Jews, but also for Christians, since Christian conversion depends on their return to their Jewish roots.

Catholic Gregory Baum makes it clear in an unambiguous statement: "After Auschwitz the Christian churches no longer wish to convert the Jews."[20] Baum gives two reasons to support this conclusion. The first reason concerns Jews, because "asking the Jews to become Christians is a spiritual way of blotting them out of existence, and thus only reinforces the effects of the Holocaust."[21] The second reason concerns Christians themselves: "After Auschwitz and the participation of the nations, it is the Christian world that is in need of conversion."[22]

The survival of Jews as Jews is then necessary not only for Jews, but also for Christians, since Christian conversion depends on their return to their Jewish roots. After Auschwitz, it is Gentile Christians who have to come back to the people of God and not the other way around. As already noted, the mission *to* the Jews has now become a mission *of* the Jews. In his comment on the recent resolution passed by the Synod of the Protestant church

---

[19] Moore, *Christian Theology after the Shoah*, 139.
[20] Gregory Baum, "Rethinking the Church's Mission after Auschwitz," in *Auschwitz: Beginning of a New Era?* (ed. E. Fleischner; New York: Ktav, 1977), 113.
[21] Ibid.
[22] Ibid.

of the Rhineland,[23] Rolf Rendtorff affirms the "impossibility of a Christian mission to the Jews" precisely on this very perspective: "The addition of the Gentiles to the people of God."[24]

Paradoxically, this principle holds even when Jews accept the Christian message; even if Jews find in Christianity the truth of God, even if they come to believe in Jesus as their Messiah, they will not like to be identified as "converts"; they will refuse to become Gentile Christians. After Auschwitz, the Jews, even Christian Jews, cannot forget that they are Jews; instead, they will still, and perhaps more than ever and more than non-Christian Jews, affirm their Jewishness and thus play an unexpected and significant role in the process of Christian conversion.

This phenomenon is new and can be observed in Christian communities where Christian Jews do not only claim their Jewish identity through their teaching and their testimony, but they also help Christians to draw closer to their Jewish roots. In this connection, the so-called Messianic Jewish movement, with 350 congregations all over the world (fifty in Israel alone), is worth noticing. For the first time in history, "Jewish people are becoming reminded of Jesus Christ in a way that they haven't been for centuries."[25] And the movement has been characterized as being "now the fastest-growing stream of faith within the Jewish community."[26] Yet, Messianic Judaism has caught Jews and Christians by surprise and has often raised suspicion, anger, and contempt on both parts. It is accused of displaying unauthentic forms of Judaism except for some artificial cosmetics such as wearing the tallith, exposing a Torah, and uttering a few Hebrew words when, in fact, many of these Jews often do not take the laws of the Torah seriously, do not keep Sabbath, do not eat kosher, and do not know Hebrew or the Jewish prayers.

It is also considered deceptive because these congregations are made of Jews and non-Jews; and yet, they present themselves as

---

[23] *Current Dialogue* 1 (Geneva: World Council of Churches, Winter 1980–81).

[24] Rolf Rendtorff, "The Effect of the Holocaust in Christian Mission to the Jews," *SIDIC* 14 (1981): 24.

[25] Gary Thomas, "The Return of the Jewish Church," *Christianity Today* 42.10 (7 September 1998): 62–69.

[26] Ibid.

"synagogues" with spiritual leaders often identified as rabbis, as if they were natural operatives of the traditional Jewish community when, in fact, they are often initiated and supported by mainline Christian churches and used as a strategy for missionizing the Jews, and their rabbis were never trained in Jewish rabbinic studies.

These are serious accusations, but they have not always been fair. The phenomenon is too recent to allow clear and impartial judgment. It has, indeed, been recognized that "there is little discussion of the place of Jewish Christians and Messianic communities."[27] Moreover, Messianic Jews have taken the lessons of the criticisms and recognized their mistakes.[28] They insist, however, that they are "legitimately part of the Jewish community," taking their "cue from the apostles, including Paul, who not only observed Jewish practices . . . but celebrated the holidays as well."[29] And building on the apostolic model, messianic congregations want to incorporate Jewish traditions in their worship and lifestyle. They use the traditional synagogue prayers, observe the Jewish holidays, light the Sabbath candles. Their congregations

> do not reflect the usual evangelical symbolism. You will not see giant crosses protruding above a baptistry, nor will you see walls of stained glass pictures of Christ and his disciples. You will rather see a candle, symbolizing the eternal light of God, just above the ark containing the Torah. To the Messianic Jew, the inclusion and placement of the Torah (the body of Jewish scriptures) in no way symbolizes bondage to the law; it is actually an expression of Jewish affinity to the laws of God, but against the backdrop of God's gracious favor in forgiving us through the Messiah's atonement.

> You will also find a departure from the traditional nineteenth-century hymns in favor of Scripture songs taken verbatim from Old and New

---

[27] Marcus Braybrooke, *Time to Meet: Towards a Deeper Relationship between Jews and Christians* (London: SCM/Phildadelphia: Trinity, 1990), 36.

[28] See Daniel C. Juster and Daniel W. Pawley, "A Messianic Jew Pleads His Case," *Christianity Today* 26.8 (24 April 1981): 22–24; Dan Cohn-Sherbok, *Messianic Judaism: The First Study of Messianic Judaism by a Non-Adherent* (New York: Continuum, 2000); and Carol Harris-Shapiro, *Messianic Judaism: A Rabbi's Journey Through Religious Change in America* (Boston: Beacon Press, 1999).

[29] John Fischer, "Messianic Jews Are Still Jews," *Christianity Today* 26.8 (24 April 1981): 25.

Testaments. The songs are often chanted; many move rhythmically with fast-paced staccato character; some flow smoothly in slightly somber minor keys. Scripture reading, prayer, and Jewish elements such as the Kiddush—a blessing and prayer over wine—interspersed with the singing, provide the structure from which spontaneous praise and worship come. This traditional Jewish worship material coalesce in harmony and unity of spirit to point to the centrality of salvation in Jesus.[30]

Therefore, in spite of all the criticism, justified or not, the experience of Messianic Judaism deserves our attention, at least for one reason: for the first time in history since the separation, Jews who become Christians vehemently refuse to define themselves as Christians "since most Jewish people associate Christians with centuries of persecution."[31] For the first time in history, Jewish Christians refuse to assimilate but instead affirm "a heartfelt identification with all the elements of history and personality that have produced the Jewish people."[32] They also deny the accusation that their operations are merely another evangelistic method to trap Jews, but are instead a sincere expression of their Jewishness. As one of them stated: "Our Jewishness is by no means an evangelistic gimmick. We choose to remain Jews because we love the Jewish people and wish to identify with them."[33]

For the first time in history since the separation, Jews who become Christians vehemently refuse to define themselves as Christians.

Again, the main reason for emphasizing their identification is found in their reference to the Holocaust. "One has to be Jewish," says the same author, "to relate in total compassion to the hearts of people who have been through the Holocaust."[34] In the past, Jews who converted lost themselves in the new Gentile Christian community and identified themselves as Christians. Today these Jews

---

[30] Juster and Pawley, "A Messianic Jew Pleads His Case," 22.
[31] Fischer, "Messianic Jews Are Still Jews," 25.
[32] Juster and Pawley, "A Messianic Jew Pleads His Case," 24.
[33] Ibid.
[34] Ibid.

want to be identified as Jews in spite of all the controversy, anger, and bewilderment they provoke. In fact, Messianic Judaism is not so much a movement about the conversion of Jews *into* Christianity, as it is often a movement of conversion *toward* Judaism. Jews who had lost their Jewish identity into Gentile Christianity, or even into secularism, through Messianic Judaism have come back to their Jewish roots.[35] And the gospel is no longer owned by Gentile Christians. Jesus is no longer a Gentile Messiah; he has returned home where he originally and naturally belongs.

And because Messianic Jews have insisted on keeping their Jewishness alive while they have opened themselves to the message of the gospel, this movement displays another new and unique feature. For the first time in history since the parting of the ways, Gentile Christians and Jewish Christians worship together and are thereby experiencing a return to the Jewish roots of Christianity.

Through the Jewish Christian it is the face of Israel that shines in the heart of Christian communities. After Auschwitz, the Jewish Christian represents an extraordinary paradox and also an amazing hope: while remaining faithful to their Jewish identity and striving to bring Gentile Christians back to their Jewish roots, Jewish Christians embody in themselves the tension and eventually the unbelievable reconciliation between Jews and Christians.

The state of Israel has also played an important role in the movement of reconciliation between Jews and Christians. From the creation of Israel, Christians have not only learned to respect the Jews, but have also discovered in the new country a source of inspiration for their Christian faith. In the past, Christians used to go to Palestine and the Middle East in order to find archaeological or historical support for their faith. Now, more and more, Christians go to Eretz Israel in order to meet with Jews, celebrate a Shabbat with them, learn Hebrew, or even attend a *yeshiva*; some go so far as to identify with their historical destiny and decide to settle there.

The importance of the Israeli contribution to biblical study, whether it concerns the Old Testament or the New Testament, the

---

[35] See Jakob Jocz, *The Jewish People and Jesus Christ after Auschwitz: A Study in the Controversy between Church and Synagogue* (Grand Rapids: Baker, 1981), 212–13.

revival of Hebrew, the intense archaeological digging of the land, and the numerous significant findings, have had a tremendous impact on the new Christian appreciation of the Jewish background of their faith. This is true on a private and personal level. But it is also true on a larger scale within professional and academic meetings and institutions. Topics such as Hebrew literature, the Holocaust, and other Jewish-related subjects are very popular. Israel has also contributed to making Christianity more Jewish: Christians are now able to nurture their religious imaginations with a more concrete reference to the real environment of their Messiah; furthermore, through Israel, Hebrew songs and traditional Jewish prayers, until now exclusively reserved to the synagogue, have been popularized and thus moved to the public domain and are now enjoyed by many Christians, who may even use them in their liturgical services.

But the creation of the state of Israel has not only affected Christians and brought them closer to Jews, it has also affected Jews and brought them closer to Christians. The Jewish movement to Christians comes as a natural response to the Christian sympathy toward them. Love generates love. But there is more. In Israel, Jews grow and

The state of Israel has, therefore, liberated the Jew from the visceral reflex of reaction to the Christian.

live for the first time in history without the daily threat of Christian anti-Semitism. Neighbors, boss, police, teachers are all Jews. The state of Israel has, therefore, liberated the Jew from the visceral reflex of reaction to the Christian. At last the Jew can freely face Jesus and ask fresh questions about him.

Furthermore, the historical and geographical situation of Israel makes the figure of Jesus present everywhere there. He is recalled in the streets of Jerusalem, in ancient tombs, and in the many churches that dot the land of Israel, in the names of the Israeli towns and villages, in Galilee and in the desert of Judea; he is mentioned in every guidebook, but also in the textbooks of every Israeli child. For the first time in history, Jesus is studied by Jews officially in an academic environment—the Hebrew University of Jerusalem has a chair in New Testament studies. Jesus is referred to by many

Christians who live in Israel and is also mentioned by Israeli guides, who have studied his words, his life, and his works. In the mouth of the Israeli, the name of Jesus has become a commonplace reference and has, therefore, lost its passionate negative connotation. Israel has drawn Jesus closer to Jews. He is now a tangible part of their geographical and historical heritage.

Christians and Jews have come closer to each other simply because they recovered their Jewish roots. The horizon of this new adventure is not clear. We should only hope that "the two Jews" would one day dare to look at each other and run the risk to witness to each other on behalf of the truth that transcends both of them.

POSTFACE: THE TWO WITNESSES

The law of Moses requires the testimony of at least two witnesses to make a report credible (Deuteronomy 17:6). In the New Testament, John repeats this principle when he states: "The testimony of two witnesses is valid" (John 8:17). Indeed when two persons tell the same story, this means that they saw the same thing. They thus confirm each other: they speak truth. Likewise the testimony of the church makes Israel a true witness, and the testimony of Israel makes the church a true witness. Both testify to the same story. The same miracles of creation, exodus, resurrection, and hope are shouted aloud, proving that God was there, he spoke and acted, that God is still there, he speaks and is alive.

This is why the two witnesses, the church *and* Israel, are needed so that people may believe and hope in something else beyond their pains and struggles and, beyond the valley of shadow, that they may bring ethics into their life and therefore become the human sign of the divine reality. The two witnesses are needed in order to repeat and thereby authenticate the same story. More, they are both needed in order to complete the story. Each witness may have seen something that escaped the other's eyes. We need both testimonies to get the whole story. Also both witnesses need each other in order to make their own story more meaningful and beautiful.

Each witness may have seen something that escaped the other's eyes.

THE CHURCH NEEDS ISRAEL

History is the first and certainly the most obvious place that makes the church dependent on Israel. The church was born and grew in the soil of Israel. The first Christians were all Jews who lived as faithful Jews. Jesus was a Jew. The Old Testament as well as the midrashim, the Jewish parables, were a part of his teachings. All his disciples were Jews; the New Testament was written by Jews who constantly referred to the Jewish Scriptures and traditions. The church needs Israel as a house needs its foundation and even more as a tree needs its roots. Karl Barth reminds Christians of this necessity: "The Church must live with the Synagogue, not, as fools say in their hearts, as with another religion or confession, but as with the root from which it stems."[1] The Apostle Paul makes this point very clearly when he compares Israel to an olive tree to which the new branches of the church were to be grafted. Note that the Jew, Paul, never spoke of a new tree that would replace the old one. For him the church was to blossom on the tree, not to replace it. The church needs Israel for its very existence and identity. But the need goes even beyond mere historical reality. The present church needs Israel for what Israel has now and what the church does not have.

The church needs the Jews in order to rediscover the intrinsic value and beauty of studying the word of God for itself.

The Hebrew Scriptures have been preserved by the tenacious work of Jewish scribes who carefully copied the ancient manuscripts and also by faithful Jews who read them throughout generations in the synagogue. Moses, Isaiah, the Psalms, the Song of Songs are still chanted today in the original language. Thanks to Israel, Christians can have access to the Hebrew text of the Old Testa-

---

[1] Quoted in Jakob Jocz, *The Jewish People and Jesus Christ after Auschwitz: A Study in the Controversy between Church and Synagogue* (Grand Rapids: Baker, 1981), 131.

ment. From the Jews, Christians will learn to pay major attention again to the Hebrew Scriptures.

Along the same lines, the church needs the Jewish people in order to rediscover the intrinsic value and beauty of studying the word of God for itself, as the word from above that has its own truth ready for discovery. The naive Christian belief that the Holy Spirit will inspire personal reading of Scripture no matter how one does it has obstructed the effort of searching Scripture for what it is. Too often the Bible has been used to prove one's point in the theological dispute or as a shallow sentimental inspiration for religious devotion.

The joy of life and the sense of the feast, the ability to receive the gift of God in creation is also a value that Christians may learn from Jews.

The Law—the Ten Commandments, the dietary laws, the Shabbat, and the whole ethical code—has not only been preserved in writing by the Jews, but it is also being witnessed to by the people who observe it in their lives. The church needs the Jews in order to rethink the theology of the law. Christians have so often stressed grace and love that they have frequently ignored the value of justice and of concrete works. Emotions and feeling and subjective experience have been overemphasized at the expense of faithfulness and will and objective duty of obedience.

The joy of life and the sense of the feast, the ability to receive the gift of God in creation is also a value that Christians may learn from Jews. From earlier stages the influence of gnosticism and especially of Marcionite Christianity has opposed faith in the God of creation to faith in the God of salvation, faith in the God of beauty and of the senses to faith in the God of the Spirit and the soul, and faith in the God of the Old Testament to faith in the God of the New Testament. And this is sometimes reflected in the Christian theology of Sunday, the sign of spiritual salvation, versus the Jewish Sabbath, the sign of the physical creation. This dualism has influenced generations of Christians and produced a religion of sadness where laughter and enjoyment are suspect. Christians could learn from

Jews to pay attention to their physical as well as their spiritual life. They could learn from them a holistic view of life. What they eat, what they drink, whatever they do affects their total being. Christians need to learn from Jews that religion is a way of life and not just a turn of the soul.

The Messiah himself would come closer to Christians if only they were closer to Jews. For many Christians the more distant and different they are from Jews, the closer they think they are to "their Lord Jesus Christ." New Testament scholar Brad Young tells this story: "In an internationally recognized university, a world-renowned New Testament scholar remarked to his students, 'The first thing you must do to be a good Christian is to kill the Jew inside of you.' One of the students raised her hand to respond to his statement with a question. The learned professor listened as she asked him, 'Do you mean Jesus?' "[2] The lesson of this story sounds loudly. If you kill the Jew, you kill Jesus; and conversely, if you make the Jew present and alive in your human and religious experience, you will then draw nearer to Jesus.

> The Messiah himself would come closer to Christians if only they were closer to Jews.

Indeed the Messiah concept is specifically Jewish. The word *christos* (Christ), from which comes the word "Christian," is nothing but the Greek translation of the Hebrew word *mashiah* (Messiah). This word is found in the Hebrew Scriptures to designate the king, the priest, the prophet, anyone who is anointed *(mashah)* by God for specific purposes. Ultimately the *mashiah* (Christ) is described in the Bible as the ideal King of David who will bring change, peace, and salvation to Israel and the world. This is why for the Jews, the Messiah has not yet come. He is expected in the future. The Christians need the Jews in order to be reminded that salvation did not take place yet, that salvation apart from the world is not salvation, that the kingdom of God is a historical, physical reality and not just an existential subjective experience. The Messiah implies hope for a

---

[2] Brad H. Young, *Jesus the Jewish Theologian* (Peabody, Mass.: Hendrickson, 1995), xxi.

better world, that is, a world that is not the one we presently know. This is why the Messiah has been represented in the Hebrew Scriptures (Numbers 24:17) and in Jewish tradition as a star, the lonely star, the last star that announces the coming of the day—the star of David, the very star emblazoned on the Israeli flag. Christians have so often emphasized the value of the past event of the crucifixion that they frequently stopped there at the cross. They do not wait anymore. They are already saved. The cross has overshadowed the star. The kingdom of God is already here. Christians could learn from Jews to become more lucid, to look around and realize that the wolf does not yet lie down with the lamb. Death, violence, suffering are still striking, eloquent signs that the Messiah is still to come. Christians could learn from Jews that the kingdom of God is not just an existential experience in the present life; it is not just a move in the heart, but it is an objective event that lies in the future and involves the physical world: "As the lightning flashes and lights up the sky from one side to the other" (Luke 17:24). With the Jews, the Christians will learn to hope.

The last, but not the least, truth that Christians could learn from Jews is the pain and ugliness of anti-Semitism. In order to abolish anti-Semitism, Christians walking closer to Jews will first expose any anti-Semitism in themselves. In the beginning, this new awareness will hit them and disturb them, and they will try to deny it, for it is not easy to recognize your iniquity. But then, they will learn how false, ridiculous, and unfair their anti-Semitic feelings and ideas were. They will discover that real Jews are nothing at all like those portrayed in their mythological imagination. Their friendly relationship and their growing familiarity with Jews will teach them the absurdity of anti-Semitism and will turn them from their flawed actions and attitudes. Not only their thoughts and their feelings will change but also their language and their vocabulary will be affected by this experience. They will become more

Christians could learn from Jews to become more lucid, to look around and realize that the wolf does not yet lie down with the lamb.

sensitive and more honest in regard to Jews. Their real relation with individual Jews will restrain them from all generalizations, such as "the Jews are like that," "that is typically Jewish," or even paradoxically, "I love the Jews." For all these expressions, including the last one, may betray conscious or unconscious anti-Semitic prejudice. The close presence of Jews will lead Christians to a radical revolution, a profound conversion. They will become more human and therefore better Christians.

ISRAEL NEEDS THE CHURCH

History has demonstrated that Israel needs the church. Christians have made the faith of Israel known throughout the earth. Thanks to Christians, the Hebrew Bible and its message have been translated into most if not all of the languages of the world. The story of Joseph and the psalms of David have been heard by Africans and by natives of the Amazon, as well as by Europeans and Americans. The particularism of Israel as a chosen people has been complemented by the universalism of the church, which took the truth of Israel beyond its historical and geographical borders. Thanks to Christians the world has learned about the existence of Israel. This is one of the most ironic and interesting paradoxes of history. Without the church the Jews might have remained a small, insignificant, and obscure religion that might well have disappeared. Rabbi Maurice Eisendrath rightly observes: "Jewish history was torn from its narrow setting in Palestine; through Christianity the Jew ceased to be a petty provincial strutting upon the narrow stage of Judea, but marched into the theater of world significance and became a blessing to all humanity. If it had not been for Christianity, Judaism and the Jew might well have remained as insignificant as have been the follow-

Without the church the Jews might have remained a small, insignificant, and obscure religion that might well have disappeared.

ers of Zoroaster."[3] The church has not only made Israel known to the nations but also made the existence of Israel necessary for the church's own existence. Israel owes its fame and survival, to some extent, to the church.

The New Testament has been largely ignored by the Jewish people, although it was written by Jews and for Jews even before the composition of the Talmud. Therefore Jews would benefit from the reading of these texts; for they not only witness to the life and belief of the first-century Jews, but they also contain valuable truths that may strengthen and enrich their Jewish roots.

The New Testament has been largely ignored by the Jewish people, although it was written by Jews and for Jews even before the composition of the Talmud.

As a matter of fact, Jews well versed in their own Scriptures and tradition may understand these writings even better than the Christians themselves do, as they often project their own Gentile worldview into them. Jews will discover that the New Testament is not as foreign as they thought, and they may even get a better grasp of their own heritage. Often the meaning and the beauty of the Hebrew Scriptures will be enhanced by the explanations of the New Testament. Also the Talmud and the midrashim will be set in context. The stories about the rabbi of Nazareth, his parables, and his teachings will surprise them by their Jewish flavor and the high Jewish ideals they convey.

Grace *(hesed)* is not specific to the Christian message. Grace is also cherished by the Jewish people. It is a genuine Jewish value. From Christians, however, Jews will be reminded that salvation is not achieved only through *mitzwoth,* but also through the God who comes down in history and acts on behalf of Israel. This teaching is not foreign to Judaism, as Pinchas Lapide notes: "The rabbinate has never considered the Torah as a way of salvation to God. . . . we Jews

---

[3] Maurice N. Eisendrath, *The Never Failing Stream* (Toronto: Macmillan, 1939), 341.

. . . regard salvation as God's exclusive prerogative, so we Jews are the advocates of 'pure grace.' "[4] Jews need to learn more about the proximity of God, the God who goes so far as to enter the complex process of incarnation in order to speak with humans, be with them, and save them. Certainly Abraham Heschel thought of this reality when he observed that "the Bible is not man's theology but God's anthropology."[5] Learning about God's incarnation, Jews will understand better the God of Abraham, Isaac, and Jacob, the God who spoke face to face with Moses, the God who fought for Israel at Jericho, the God of the prophets. And this perspective will even bring new life into their *mitzwoth*. The law will not just be performed as a required duty or as a burdensome chore; it will blossom from the heart as a fruit emerging from their personal relationship with God.

The Messiah embodies this very principle of God's involvement in human history and existence. The Christian emphasis may well therefore help the Jew to recognize the effective presence of God in the flesh of history. For the Messiah was not only to be in heaven or in the far future. He was also to be here among humans—"Messiah for all generations"—as it has been taught in mystical Judaism and recently pointed out in Hasidic currents.[6] Significantly, the Messiah is not only represented as a star in biblical and Jewish traditions, he is also expected as a human seed *(zera)* from which will come the one who will kill the serpent (Genesis 3:15)[7] or as a human sprout *(tsemah)* raised to David, who will bring salvation and safety to Israel (Jeremiah 23:5–6).

The idea of a suffering God and a suffering Messiah is found not only in the Hebrew Scriptures, but also in many ancient Jewish writings.[8] It is not a Christian invention to justify the Christian

---

[4] Pinchas Lapide and Peter Stuhlmacher, *Paul: Rabbi and Apostle* (Minneapolis: Augsburg, 1984), 37–38.

[5] Abraham Heschel, *Man Is Not Alone: A Philosophy of Religion* (New York: Octagon, 1972), 129.

[6] See Eliyahu Touger, *Sound the Great Shofar* (Brooklyn: Kehot, 1992), 20.

[7] See Etan Levine, *The Aramaic Version of the Bible: Contents and Context* (Berlin: de Gruyter, 1988), 212.

[8] See, for instance, *Sanhedrin* 98b; *Pesiqta Rabbati, Pisqa* 37; and *Bereshit Rabbati of Moshe Hadarshan* on Genesis 24:67.

view of the Messiah. Yet the Christians are those who preserved it and emphasized it. As a result, many Jews reacted to it and looked at it with suspicion. Contact with Christians will therefore help Jews to rediscover this truth as an original datum of the Jewish heritage.

With the Christians, the Jews will also learn about Jesus. They will discover that he is not what they thought he was. They will be intrigued by him; they will hear him confirming their Jewish commitment. They will honor him. They will then understand that redemption is not just a future event located in the cosmic and political arena; it is also enrooted in the hearts: "The kingdom of God is among you" (Luke 17:21) and carries a present dimension. From Christians, the Jews

They will realize that through Jesus the God of Israel has become the God of all nations and the religion of Israel has become a universal religion.

may learn about the proximity of God and live the experience of a personal relationship with him. They will rediscover the earnestness of the religion of love that springs out of God's movement toward humankind. They will realize that through Jesus the God of Israel has become the God of all nations and the religion of Israel has become a universal religion (Zechariah 14:9).

TWO VOICES FOR THE SAME GOD

Both witnesses, Israel and the church, are needed—not only because they confirm each other's truth, but also because each one brings a truth, a dimension, that is ignored or simply rejected by the other. They need each other; they are complementary. This thesis was initiated in the early twentieth century by Jewish theologian Franz Rosenzweig in his *Star of Redemption* and was even suggested to a certain extent by Jewish philosopher Martin Buber in his *Two Faiths*. Today, in the post-Holocaust era, this direction of thinking is more and more advocated by Christian and Jewish theologians as well.

Lately, Catholic theologian Hans Küng made this revolutionary statement: "What *seems to be* divisive has to be reexamined in a self-critical way. Take the example of the preexistence of Christ . . . I think we have to discuss what the real differences are: the Law, the State of Israel, etc."[9] Jewish theologian Michael Wyschogrod invited Jews to be more open to the idea of the incarnation of God since "the biblical God is also very human";[10] and he called "Christians to accept the obligatory nature of Torah commandments . . . even after Jesus."[11] Wyschogrod then describes the two-way process: "As Christians deepen their understanding of Christianity's Jewish roots, Jews must try to understand Christianity's role in God's redemptive work."[12] Likewise, Rabbi Hershel Matt sees Christianity and Judaism "as the two vehicles of God's revelation: in one case, the *People* Israel, bearers of the Torah; in the other case, the *Person* of Christ, one-man embodiment of Israel and the Torah. Through their respective vehicles, Judaism and Christianity affirm, God makes known His word and will and way, His resources and even His indwelling presence."[13] This is a remarkable recognition.

One of the most eloquent declarations was given a few years ago by Protestant theologian Mark Fressler in a speech at Auschwitz: "The Jews witness to the absolute transcendence which founds all ethics, the law. The Christians witness to the incarnation of the Word. Two voices for the same God! Two different voices whose harmony is promised beyond the times."[14] Israel and the church should indeed be heard as "two voices for the same God."

The voice of Israel witnesses to Christians about the Torah and the requirement of righteousness; the call for justice and holiness; the importance of revering, searching, and listening to the written

---

[9] James H. Charlesworth, "Discussing Anti-Judaism in the New Testament with Hans Küng," *Explorations* 6.2 (1992): 2.

[10] Michael Wyschogrod, "A Jewish View of Christianity," in *Toward a Theological Encounter: Jewish Understandings of Christianity* (ed. Leon Klenicki; New York: Paulist, 1991), 114.

[11] Ibid., 119.

[12] Ibid.

[13] Hershel J. Matt, "How Shall a Believing Jew View Christianity?" *Judaism* 24 (1975): 395.

[14] Quoted in Albert Nicolas, "Le dialogue judéo-chrétien à l'heure de vérité," *Le christianisme du XXème siècle* (April 1991): 14.

word of God; the truth and beauty of the Holy Scriptures; the value of creation and the enjoyment of life; the celebration of time in the experience of the weekly Shabbat; the particularist perspective of God's covenant with his people; the "not yet" of the messianic hope.

The voice of the church witnesses to Jews about the event of God's salvation; his visitation in the flesh of human history; the awareness of human misery and iniquity; the good news of God's grace and love to humankind; the call for love and forgiveness; the proximity of God; his personal relationship with each individual; the universalistic perspective of God's covenant with humankind; the "already" of the kingdom of God.

The voice of Israel witnesses to Christians about the Torah and the requirement of righteousness. . . . The voice of the church witnesses to Jews about the event of God's salvation.

When these two witnesses, the "two Jews" of Israel Zangwill, hear each other as the voice of the *same* God—then, at last, the voice of God will be heard.

INDEX OF NAMES AND SUBJECTS

INDEX OF ANCIENT SOURCES

1:17   2
1:21   2
4:18   9
5:17   14
5:18–20   15
5:20   15
5:21–22, 27–28   15
8:13   5
9:9   9
9:20   4
10:5–6   73
11:29   12
15:31   11
21:10–11   27
21:45–46   24
22:19–22   7
22:37–40   5
23   7
23:2–3   14
23:5   4
26:3–5   24
26:31   25
26:38   12
26:49   4
27:1   25
27:25   27
27:46   3
27:57–61   7

Mark
1:1   13
5:41   3
7:27   73
7:28   73
8:36   12
10:1   23
12:12   24
12:30   12
14:1   24
14:2   24, 25
14:34   12
14:36   3
15:13   25

Luke
1:46   12
1:68   11
2:212
2:41–43   3
2:41–47   3

3:38   13
4:14–15   23
4:16–20   3
6:15   9
9:30–31   7
11:8   5
11:39–54   7
17:21   97
17:24   93
19:47   24
19:48   23, 24
21:38   23
22:2   24
23:14   25
23:34   27
24:27   10

John
1:1   13
1:38   4
3:1   9
5:39   10
8:17   89
9:22   36
11:45–50   25
12:42   36
13:34   21
19:15   25
19:39–40   7
20:16   4

Acts
2   28
2:14, 22, 29, 36,
   42–47   73
2:41   12, 28
2:47   28
3   28
4   28
4:4   28
4:32   28
5:16   28
6:7   9, 28
6:9–8:2   34
9:1–17   28
9:20–21   29
9:22   29
9:31   29
11   29
11:19   29

11:21   29
12:2   34
13:5   29
13:15   29
13:17, 23   11
13:43–44   29
14   29
14:1   29
15   19, 20, 29, 75
15:2   20
15:5   29
15:20–21   20
15:28–29   20
21:20   29
24:5   35
28:17   30
28:21   30
28:22   30
28:23   30
28:30   30
28:31   30

Romans
1:16   73
2:9   12
2:28–29   22
3:31   17
4:15   16
6:17   16
7:22   16
8:15–17   16
9:4–5   11, 71
11:18   56, 71

1 Corinthians
15:3   10

2 Corinthians
3:6, 14   64

Colossians
2:17   18

2 Timothy
3:16   10

Hebrews
1.1–2   11
4:8   2
8:5   18